DON'T WORRY ABOUT THE ROBOTS

DON'T WORRY ABOUT THE ROBOTS

HOW TO SURVIVE AND THRIVE IN THE NEW WORLD OF WORK

**Dr Jo Cribb &
David Glover**

ALLEN&UNWIN
SYDNEY • MELBOURNE • AUCKLAND • LONDON

First published in 2018

Copyright © Jo Cribb and David Glover, 2018

Allen & Unwin
Level 3, 228 Queen Street
Auckland 1010, New Zealand
Phone: (64 9) 377 3800
Email: info@allenandunwin.com
Web: www.allenandunwin.co.nz

83 Alexander Street
Crows Nest NSW 2065, Australia
Phone: (61 2) 8425 0100

A catalogue record for this book is available from the
National Library of New Zealand.

ISBN 978 1 760633 50 9

Design by Kate Barraclough
Set in Tiempos Text 10.5/17pt

Cover images by Josef Kubes (front) and Mauro Rodrigues (back), Shutterstock.com

Printed and bound in Australia by Griffin Press
10 9 8 7 6 5 4

To our life partners, Mike and Yvonne,
for their loving support and patience, and
our children, who are the future of work.

I am a great believer in luck. The harder
I work, the more of it I seem to have.

—COLEMAN COX

He mahi te ataa noho, e kii ana te wheke
It is the octopus who says sitting is working.

—MĀORI PROVERB

Man who stands on a hill with mouth open will
wait a long time for roast duck to drop in.

—CONFUCIUS

CONTENTS

FOREWORD

by Dame Wendy Pye DNZM, MBE

 During the 50 years of my working life, I have seen many changes in the way we work, the way we communicate and the way we gather information. I am excited to see how David and Jo use interviews with smart people to challenge ideas about where we are going, and to give readers the opportunity to explore creative ways to determine their futures. The important message is that, though change is often difficult, it is only through accepting change and fresh approaches that you achieve results.

Today we live our lives linked with a much wider audience than in the past, via our phones and the internet, with the exchange of messages, news and information during every waking moment. How different life was when we had a mailing system, followed by the telex and later the fax machine. The working week ended on a Friday, and you got feedback on Monday. Manuscripts and artwork were sent via courier to a printer in Hong Kong. Now the files are sent via a computer network in seconds.

I recall when the company I was working for installed a fax machine. It occupied a special locked room in the New Zealand Newspaper Office. You had to get a key from the CEO's personal assistant to send a fax, and you had to justify your reason for sending it. In the early eighties I went overseas to visit our partners in the US. I convinced them that the fax was the future, and though they were unsure, they made the necessary investment of over $5000. Today faxes are museum pieces, as are CD-ROMs—all this in the past few decades.

> I recall when the company I was working for installed a fax machine. It occupied a special locked room in the New Zealand Newspaper Office. You had to get a key from the CEO's personal assistant to send a fax, and you had to justify your reason for sending it.

In the late nineties, I made the decision to create a print programme and simultaneously launch it on a digital platform with animation and extension activities. (At the time you dialled up to access digital content!) I wanted to develop a total reading programme in digital format and sell this to the world for $50. I had seen how PlayStations were having an impact and I imagined that the telcos would be enthusiastic about delivering this dream. After considerable investment, and with the help of clever New Zealand software designers and educationalists, I went out to the world to share this project. British Telecom said video would never play on the internet. Singtel in Singapore listened but did not understand.

New Zealand Telecom gave me a cold cup of coffee.

The only player was Telstra in Australia, so together we launched a package for parents. This product became Sunshine Online, which is used by thousands of children every day, both web-based and as an app, and now preloaded on a tablet. Following the success of this experiment I also launched a learning programme for preschoolers that was delivered via cable by TimeWarner in the US.

**The human connection is still important
to achieve business success.**

Today our web- and app-based literacy programmes track individual student progress and feed back vital information to teachers about the achievements of their students. This way of delivering learning is especially important for disadvantaged children and those struggling with the language of their adoptive country. Touch screens have meant this content is now easily used by small children. Tablets are in classrooms all over the world. Teachers use the internet for professional training and finding new and clever ways to direct classroom learning. Our challenge today in literacy education is to ensure that we make the most of the communication systems available to us without impacting negatively on the role of the good teacher.

The human connection is also still important to achieve business success. I do a great deal of negotiation via Skype and emails, but still there is a need to visit and talk person-to-person about a deal, particularly in the Asian markets. People still like to sit down together, as we all do as families, and talk about the deal and ways to work together over a good meal and good wine.

People around the world often ask me why, when I am in my seventies, I still work, developing ways to help children around the world learn to read. For me, when the sun comes up there is always a new idea and a new plan to work with and develop. I do hope the footprint I leave will have made a difference to the lives of many children. With over 300 million copies of our Sunshine Books, there is someone, somewhere, today reading a Sunshine story that is making a difference to their literacy learning and love of reading.

Don't be afraid of the future. If you have a dream, try it out. Make sure it is practical and works financially for you. I go out on the road and sell and sell again. Once I have found the right person to deal with, I share my dream with them and find out what their dream is. I am persistent. I never sell myself or my product short for short-term gain. I want an evergreen product that will last, but I am always open to new ideas that will improve it.

I am sure this book will provide inspiration for you, the reader, to develop new ways of thinking and achieve great enjoyment and success in whatever you choose to do. Good luck for your future.

Dame Wendy Pye DNZM, MBE
Exceptional Services to Entrepreneurship Award, 2017
Honorary Doctorate of Education (Massey University), 2018

INTRODUCTION

'Forty per cent of jobs to disappear in the next 20 years!' 'Robots to replace humans!' 'The end of the nine-to-five working day!'

Every day we seem to read headlines that forecast a grim future for employment as we know it, amid speculation about which industries will be disrupted next. Commentators seize on expert opinion that claims we are facing a depressing readjustment in the size and nature of the global workforce, and that many of us will soon be past our use-by dates.

But what's really going on here and, just as importantly, what can we do about it? How can we prepare ourselves for the changes that will occur in the workforce in the coming years?

This project started with a conversation we had about work in early 2017. Jo had just left the safety of a high-flying career in the civil service. David was contemplating his next move after several years of running a business consultancy. We talked about the wide range of choices that young people face, and the conflicting messages they receive about their futures. We discussed what was happening to our friends and colleagues, and the impact of technology-driven changes that were rewriting the rules around jobs and sustainable careers. We both knew people who were being made redundant through continual restructuring, while others were choosing to leave the regular workforce to set up their own businesses or work across a number of roles. We knew people who were too scared to risk making any change, working long and unsustainable hours, in denial about what might happen to their jobs in the long term. We pondered the concept of career, and how the very idea of 'retirement' was changing as people worked longer and in different ways.

It seemed to us that the biggest risk was to remain passive in the face of all these developments, and to expect the future to be simply a more hi-tech version of the present. We could see that our own skills needed to be sharpened and refreshed if we were to continue to flourish in the new environment. When we began to investigate further we found that while there is a lot of information available about the future of work, there seemed to be very little about what individual workers could do to prepare for that future. How should people start to respond to change? Which examples of success can they look to? What are the practical steps they can take to ensure they have a viable and enjoyable future working life?

Taking charge of the future

Our aim in writing this book is simple. We want New Zealanders to start taking charge of their future of work—to explore what is happening in their industries and organisations, to judge the impact this will have on them personally, and to take proactive steps to prepare themselves and their families for change.

The book brings together the experience and insights that we and others have gained over our careers, and distils these into practical ideas about how to manage the high-speed changes ahead of us. Integral to the book are the voices of twelve New Zealanders who have created interesting, vital careers. These people have a variety of backgrounds and work in diverse fields, and they have a range of views on what the future holds and how to move forward effectively. We selected these particular people because they are doing what we think all New Zealanders need to do. They are exploring what is happening around them, working out what it means for them personally, and taking action accordingly.

As these people shared their insights and achievements, they inspired us with their confidence and their varied approaches. We also uncovered some common themes and approaches that worked well, and we realised that while some of the technologies may be new, our best response is often what has always helped humans as we face new challenges: curiosity, confidence, experimentation and learning.

While the nature of work is undoubtedly changing quickly, this book is based on the belief that the future doesn't have to mean bad news. We may look back in twenty years with amusement or nostalgia as we recollect how we used to live and what we considered to be worthwhile careers, but if we provide ourselves with both the skill set and the mindset to move with the times, we really don't have to worry about the robots.

If we are willing to let go of our normal patterns of behaviour and traditional assumptions, we can embark on a journey of discovery and make the most of the opportunities that present themselves. Having pushed ourselves beyond our comfort zones and taken a clear look at ourselves and the world around us, we can face whatever that world throws at us with increased confidence. We can survive and thrive.

Introducing David

Before you go any further you might want to know a bit more about us, and what makes us think we are qualified to offer advice about the future of work. Jo and I have quite different backgrounds, but we have both had broad experience of executive and governance work which has enabled us to develop insights into all kinds of different workplaces. I have enjoyed two distinct careers: the first in advertising, and the second in education. I have worked around the world with multinational companies, started and owned several businesses, and consulted to government, business and not-for-profit organisations. I have been a director of various companies since the age of 23, and I am on the boards of several education technology companies. My day job entails being part of the leadership team at Unitec, New Zealand's largest institute of technology.

Unlike some of the people we interviewed for the book, I have never had a definitive game plan for my career, but always tried to stay open to the next step. After a decade of working in London I secured a job in Australia, then moved on to Indonesia and finally New Zealand. This physical disruption every few years has not always been easy. When you move frequently both between sectors and geographically you experience a lack of continuity, and it is harder to know where you fit and to build something of lasting value. But you also realise that today and tomorrow are always more important than yesterday, and you learn the power of flexibility and resilience.

A lot of my work has involved taking a strategic view of the future and mapping out the possibilities. While it is not possible to predict or control all of life's outcomes, I believe you can prepare yourself to manage better whatever comes along. You do not know in advance the really big things that will drive or disrupt your career. They come from outside and are generally beyond your control, whether for good or bad. It is how you respond that determines your success.

As a coach and mentor to staff, colleagues and clients I tend to take the optimistic approach and encourage experimentation and getting out of your comfort zone. I have learned that it is better to do something than to die wondering. Most failures are not permanent—there is always a next thing you can do. It just might not be what you planned.

Introducing Jo

Like David, I have had two careers, with a side-step in the middle of the first. After completing my Master's degree—living in Samoa and studying attitudes to family violence—I had a number of social policy roles in government agencies, working on issues from community funding to job creation schemes. I was appointed to my first management job at the tender age of 27.

Realising that a large and demanding leadership role was, for me, incompatible with having children, I enrolled in full-time study for a PhD. My son arrived at the end of my first year of research and I graduated, heavily pregnant with my daughter, 21 months later. Study gave me the flexibility to adjust to being a mum while still working on issues about which I cared deeply, and to remain connected to work. I was planned in my approach to work and had a series of progressively larger management roles, including leading child poverty work at the Office of the Children's Commissioner and later as Chief Executive of the Ministry for Women.

My second career began in late 2016 when I chose to start my own consulting business. I purposely stepped off the traditional career ladder to concentrate on the issues I care deeply about—developing women leaders, gender equality, literacy and poverty, and the capability of the non-government organisation (NGO) sector. This has taken a lot of pressure off my family life and ensured I have time for looking after my health. As a result, I am more balanced and happy.

The consulting business has now evolved into a portfolio career. I have taken on leading an NGO part-time, and a number of directorships, as well as coaching women leaders and consulting to government agencies, NGOs and companies.

How to use this book

This book is designed so that you can dip into the parts that interest you or read it straight through—whichever works for you. Each chapter explores a major topic and offers practical advice. We have written some of the chapters jointly and some individually—in the latter cases the author is indicated with 'by David' or 'by Jo' underneath the chapter title. There are also sections on each of our interviewees, in which they share their stories in their own words.

Chapter 1: Work, but not as we know it
The first chapter provides an overview of what is happening to the world of work, particularly as it is challenged and changed by developments in new technologies. Are the robots really

going to take our jobs? What are the new jobs that will be worth having? What does all this mean for the workers of the future?

Chapter 2: Four key technology-driven trends

In the second chapter we get more specific and identify four major trends that are already impacting on the world of work and our responses. What effects is automation having? What's the gig economy? How is learning changing, and policy being developed to help deal with all this disruption?

The next four chapters explore key principles that will enable you to disrupt yourself in a positive way so that you are able to survive and thrive in the new world of work.

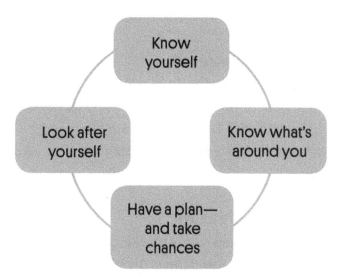

Chapter 3: Know yourself

In this chapter we discuss the importance of really knowing yourself, and ways in which you can do this. Where have you come from? What are your drivers? Do you understand your values, your *why*? What is your personal brand? How do you respond to failure, and rebound with confidence?

Chapter 4: Know what's around you

We explore the need to be aware of what's around you, and how you can increase your knowledge and connect with opportunities that will help you be successful. How curious are you? How do you keep track of what's coming? What's the value of networking, coaches and mentors? How do you find the networking technique that best suits your personality?

Chapter 5: Have a plan—and take chances

This chapter is all about looking forward and taking action in a deliberate and organised way. What's your plan and how will you make it happen? How open are you to changes along the way? How hard are you willing to work?

Chapter 6: Look after yourself

Looking after yourself physically, mentally and emotionally is vital if you are to thrive in the new world of work. Are you investing in yourself? Do you know how to manage life and work? What are the best ways to stay positive and build resilience?

Chapter 7: Bring on the future

The final chapter issues you with the challenge of acting on what you have learnt throughout the book. Our interviewees offer some advice on what they think are the most important things they have learnt from their experience of work, and we end with a reminder that humans have always faced, and survived, change.

Details of all the sources we mention in the text are provided in the Notes, while the Select Bibliography lists the most significant sources and some additional texts for further reading.

Twelve smart people who know how to survive and thrive

In deciding whose voices we wanted to include in the book, we set out to find people who have a success mindset, are open to learning, and have chosen work that is true to who they are and the values they hold. They had to be willing to share with us highlights of their life/work journey, as well as lessons they had learnt along the way, and together they needed to bring a range of answers to the question 'How do you survive and thrive in the new world of work?'

We wanted people who were achieving interesting things, often in unusual ways. We wanted to represent a range of ages, work sectors and cultures, but also capture ideas to which we could all potentially relate. Importantly, we wanted to collect practical advice based on real experience. Our aim is to be as helpful to someone who is about to leave school or university as to an experienced worker wondering where to go next, or to older workers re-evaluating their need to work.

The twelve smart people we selected include, among other things, futurists, entrepreneurs, scientists, a poet and a lawyer. These are the voices you will be hearing throughout the rest of the book.

 **Brian Steele** has a portfolio career involving governance roles, strategic projects and investment banking through his business Shoreline Partners. With both an accounting and an arts degree, he brings business rigour to his passion for linking business and the community. He believes curiosity is a driving force in his career.

Dan Khan was a software programmer until he became involved in leading New Zealand's emerging technology start-up scene. His company ZeroPoint Ventures provides early-stage funding and coaching for entrepreneurs, and he is fascinated by the challenges of establishing and growing a business.

Frances Valintine is an education futurist and the founder and Chair of The Mind Lab by Unitec and Tech Futures Lab. She helps schoolchildren, teachers and businesspeople successfully engage with the digital tools of the future.

Holona Lui runs Catalyst Pacific, a business that helps organisations communicate effectively across cultures for high performance. Drawing on strong Pacific cultural values, he helps people build better teams and personal working relationships in a range of cross-cultural environments.

Joshua Vial is an entrepreneur and programmer, and co-founder of social enterprise Enspiral and education business Enspiral Dev Academy. He is passionate about developing a better, faster way to educate future students.

Linda Clark was one of New Zealand's leading political journalists before she retrained as a lawyer. She draws on her unique combination of legal and communication skills and in-depth understanding of the political environment to help clients find the most pragmatic and cost-effective solutions to their problems.

Dr Michelle Dickinson is a nanotechnologist and science educator based at the University of Auckland. She is also known as Nanogirl. Michelle has always followed her dreams and never let traditional stereotypes scare her. She strongly believes that everyone should have access to learning about science and how things work, no matter what their age or education level.

Rachel Petero is an entrepreneur, coach and professional speaker, and founded Rise2025 to promote the leadership aspirations of indigenous women. Her ambition is to have a positive impact on 100,000 indigenous women and girls by 2025.

Rachel Taulelei is CEO of food and beverage company Kono and an award-winning entrepreneur. With her passion for the primary sector, she has a strong commitment to creating values-based business models focused on the sustainability of natural resources.

Associate Professor Selina Tusitala Marsh is a Pasifika poet and scholar who lectures in creative writing and Māori and Pacific literary studies. She was the first Pasifika person to graduate with a PhD in English from the University of Auckland. Selina is currently New Zealand's Poet Laureate.

Shay Wright is a young entrepreneur who has quickly gained recognition for his leadership and innovative approaches. He is helping to rebuild the local Māori economy through education, with his business Te Whare Hukahuka.

Vivien Maidaborn is chief executive of UNICEF NZ and has spent her career working in the community, disability and health sectors. She is also actively involved in the entrepreneurial space through her work with social enterprise Loomio.

CHAPTER 1:
WORK, BUT NOT AS WE KNOW IT

For centuries people have used their creativity and powers of invention to develop new tools and technologies to make their lives easier. Significant innovations have been created, and in time each has been superseded by a new technological development. The clothes mangle, the slide rule, the VCR, the CD—each of these was a major innovation in its time. The washing machine's spin cycle eventually put paid to the mangle, while the slide rule was replaced by the pocket calculator, until that was itself overtaken by free phone apps. The VCR is unknown to the current generation of primary school children, and even the CD is ancient history for them. Once new technologies have been adopted they quickly become taken for granted. It is the new possibilities that continue to fascinate and challenge us.

Back in the 1980s, computer scientist Alan Kay observed that 'technology is anything that wasn't around when you were born'. What has changed in recent years is the pace of change itself. Fuelled by the exponential development of computer speed and power, and increased global competition to offer new products and services, whole industries are dramatically reinventing themselves and their work practices.

In 2016 the number of applications for international patents—a leading indicator of new inventions on the horizon—hit a record of 233,000, a 7.3 per cent increase on the previous year. Digital communications and computer technology showed the greatest activity by sector.[1] Inevitably, the arrival of new digitally enhanced technologies will threaten the existence of some jobs and even whole industries. Many commentators believe that during the next few decades we will experience the biggest disruption to employment in human history.

The Fourth Industrial Revolution

Professor Klaus Schwab is the founder and executive chairman of the World Economic Forum (WEF), which studies global issues affecting education and the workplace. He has described a future he calls the Fourth Industrial Revolution.

The First Industrial Revolution occurred in the nineteenth century, when water and steam power were used to mechanise production and distribution, affecting industries such as cotton, and developments like railway networks. The Second Industrial Revolution, in the early twentieth century, harnessed electric power for mass production and led to the development of assembly lines. The Third Industrial Revolution, which began around the 1970s, featured mainframe computers, personal computing and the arrival of the internet. Now, with the digital revolution being extended and a host of new innovations emerging from science labs and computer research centres, we are entering the Fourth Industrial Revolution.

Unlike previous industrial revolutions, which created as many jobs as they destroyed, Schwab believes this latest era will be profoundly challenging. In 2016 the WEF predicted that current trends 'could lead to a net employment impact of more than 5.1 million jobs lost to disruptive labour market changes over the period 2015–2020'.[2]

The revolution is already upon us. The reason is the speed with which science and technology are now moving from the laboratory to the workplace. Innovations in fields such as nanotechnology, 3-D printing, artificial intelligence and machine learning, robotics and genetics are rapidly being exploited and applied by business and government sectors alike. As these fields are combined, widespread disruption to labour markets across the world is beginning to occur.

> In 2016 the WEF predicted that current trends 'could lead to a net employment impact of more than 5.1 million jobs lost to disruptive labour market changes over the period 2015–2020'.

As the WEF notes: 'a tangible impact of many of these disruptions on the adequacy of employees' existing skill sets can already be felt in a wide range of jobs and industries today. Given the rapid pace of change, business model disruptions are resulting in a near-simultaneous impact on skill sets for both current and emerging jobs across industries.'[3]

What does this mean in practical terms? In 2013, academics Carl Benedikt Frey and Michael A. Osborne wrote, 'according to our estimates, about 47 per cent of total US employment is at risk'. Jobs that could be computerised would disappear, and wage levels for the remaining jobs would reduce.[4]

Closer to home, in 2015, Chartered Accountants Australia and New Zealand and the New Zealand Institute of Economic Research published a report titled *Disruptive Technologies*, in which they predicted that almost half of all jobs are at risk of being automated over the next two decades, with rural New Zealand being hit the hardest.[5] Those most at risk were identified as labourers, machinery operators and drivers, and clerical and administrative roles, which currently involve over 370,000 jobs.

It's not all bad news

It may not all be bad news. The World Bank, not generally known for excessive optimism, expressed a more positive view in a report entitled *Digital Dividends*, in which it stated: 'The internet supports job creation and makes workers more productive. People have an enormous desire to communicate and connect. The personal welfare gains from having access to digital technology are clearly great.'[6]

There are other perspectives in which technology's possibilities are positively embraced, and people who are excited about the potential to extend human capability. Disruptive education business Singularity University, for example, aims to empower individuals and organisations 'with the mindset, skillset, and network to build breakthrough solutions that leverage emerging technologies like artificial intelligence, robotics, and digital biology'.[7]

Simon Raik-Allen, the former chief technology officer at

the Australian accounting software company MYOB, told the Stuff news organisation in 2016 that the blending of biology and technology to provide physical and mental enhancements to humans is inevitable: 'Imagine a version of today's app store—the brain-app store or the body-app store—which you can connect to in order to download the latest developments in intelligence, mental performance, or simply entertainment. Got an important business meeting in China? Download the language app and speak like a local with an accent add-on.'[8]

Canadian learning consultant Harold Jarche foresees an encouraging new direction for us as human beings: 'We cannot become more efficient than machines. All we can do is be more curious, more creative, more empathetic. The fact that automation is taking away jobs once designed for people means that it is time we focus on what is really important; our humanity.'[9]

We agree with Jarche, which is why this book focuses on real people who are successfully navigating the challenges in their working lives. While our interviewees differ from each other in many ways, they all share the qualities of curiosity, creativity and empathy.

Mark Osborne, Senior Advisor at New Zealand company CORE Education, makes the point simply and clearly: 'Humans are moving from working with their hands and their back, as craftsmen and artisans, to working with their head and their heart, applying creativity and problem-solving.'[10]

Workers of the future

So what exactly does this mean for the workers of the future? And what should we say to our children, our grandchildren, our nieces and nephews or our neighbours' kids when they ask us how they should prepare for their futures in work?

It is clear that what London Business School professors Lynda Gratton and Andrew Scott call a 'three-stage life'[11]—spending the first phase in education, then working in a series of roles with increasing responsibility, then retiring—is becoming unlikely for the current generation of workers, let alone those that follow. In their book *The 100-Year Life*, Gratton and Scott suggest that the reality for those who are just setting out on the journey of work will be a long working life, perhaps a decade or more than previous generations, and a long retirement because they will live longer.

Rather than slogging it out working for 50 years, it will be normal to have periods of retraining, self-employment and part-time work as well as periods working for others. Even today, many workers are continuing to work in some form well past the age of 65, and younger workers expect to have periods of retraining and self-employment as well as working on the career ladder.

The workers of the future will need to be agile and flexible to meet the demands of the market, their own personal needs, changing attitudes to work and exponential changes in technology. Research published in 2017 by the Foundation for Young Australians shows that the model of a traditional linear career is fast becoming antiquated;[12] today's fifteen-year-old is predicted to have seventeen different jobs across five careers in their lifetime. Today's preschoolers will likely have many more.

The Foundation forecasts that by 2030 there will be a reduction in the need for workers to undertake routine and manual tasks. Instead they will need to spend more time solving problems, focusing on people and thinking creatively.

The Foundation even goes so far as to point out that the workers of the future will spend 30 per cent more time learning on the job. They will need to be good thinkers because they will spend 100 per cent more time solving problems, 41 per cent more time in critical thinking and judgement, 77 per cent more time using science and maths skills, and 17 per cent more time using their communication and interpersonal skills. Employers of the future will increasingly demand these types of skills rather than specific technical skills.

By 2030 there will be a reduction in the need for workers to undertake routine and manual tasks. Instead they will need to spend more time solving problems, focusing on people and thinking creatively.

Interestingly, the same researchers predict changes in the way organisations of the future will run. Workers will need to develop an entrepreneurial mindset as work is increasingly driven through digital platforms rather than management. They will work without a manager for three hours more per week than currently, and 14 per cent less time will be used for organisation co-ordination and 10 per cent less for teaching staff. The workers of the future will need to be more self-directing and self-motivated.

Young people will need to be smart learners. New data and technology will constantly change how jobs are done. Workers will need to use learning to acquire new skills and update their knowledge (carrying out tasks like learning how to use new apps or developing new technical skills) and to analyse and interpret information (such as developing insights from data or interpreting consumer demand). Learning is likely to involve not only formal education but also on-the-job training and experiential learning (learning by doing). In addition to acquiring technical skills, young people will need to focus on developing broader skills such as communication and problem-solving that they will use across many of their roles.

Young people will need to be smart thinkers. Foundation skills of maths and science will matter, but it will be the application of these skills that is important. Doctors, for example, will need to use their maths and science knowledge for diagnostic tasks (such as processing and analysing information and developing a plan). They will also increasingly need to focus on communication—interpreting information for others, communicating their thoughts, providing advice and caring for others. Workers of the future will spend more time sharing their ideas, learning and problem-solving. Their work will involve more interpersonal interaction.

Young people will need to be smart doers. With less management, workers will need to be more autonomous and work independently. More people will work from home, and they will need to manage their time and prioritise tasks more effectively. They will need to motivate themselves, as there will not be someone looking over their shoulder to make sure they are working.

The Foundation for Young Australians argues that we should focus on equipping young people with the right skills rather than focusing on actual jobs, and advocates for early-career work experience that is broad and focused on building a wide range of skills. It is suggested that young people should be encouraged to become comfortable with changing employers and occupations multiple times. They should think about their careers as clusters of jobs that they are interested in and build on their strengths rather than focus on one dream job.

When a person trains or works in one job, they acquire the skills for thirteen other jobs.

Some clusters have stronger future prospects than others. Those based on manual and routine tasks (admissions clerks, florists, mechanics) have the weakest prospects. Those that are strong involve providing advice and solutions (HR advisors, policy advisors, statisticians) or caring functions (nurses, tour guides, social workers) or technology improvements (web developers, programmers).[13]

Interestingly, when analysing job clusters through the lens of the skills gained, these researchers found that jobs are often more related than we realise. When a person trains or works in one job, they acquire the skills for thirteen other jobs. Underlying all roles, however, is the need to prepare our young people with the skills to work independently and entrepreneurially. Gaining skills that are portable across jobs in a cluster is important. Critical thinking, for example, is likely to be a key skill across many job clusters. Seeking out job clusters where they can increase and demonstrate this skill will hold workers in good stead across a wide range of clusters and roles.

As the world of work changes, so new stages of life may evolve as well. Teenagers were 'invented' in the mid-twentieth century as childhood and education became extended. Perhaps we will see a new category—those who have finished formal education but are still experimenting and have not yet settled into work as an established life phase—the extended-gap-year-agers? Perhaps mid-career (in their late forties) people will need to take a breather, and this might become another new life phase—the mid-life Overseas Experience perhaps?

The fact is that many of the technology-driven changes in the world of work are happening already. Many employers are already demanding that workers have ability in critical thinking, interpersonal skills, communication skills, problem-solving and science and maths capability. This is across most jobs, not just those that have traditionally required university qualifications. The Foundation for Young Australians' analysis of online job ads showed there was an increase of over 200 per cent in demand for digital skills over the past three years, while the demand for critical thinking increased over 150 per cent.[14] A Finnish research report published in 2015 mapped the volume of company restructurings in Europe.[15] Over the past few years, tens of thousands of workers had been involved in almost constant restructuring of their companies.

It is not only the children of today who face a new world of work—today's workers also need to be reassessing their roles and taking action to ensure they are able to thrive in this new environment.

CHAPTER 2:
FOUR KEY TECHNOLOGY-DRIVEN TRENDS

We know that technology is changing rapidly, and that our lives are already being affected in numerous ways. But before we look at how we can create successful working lives in this changing environment, let's consider the specifics of the changes that are taking place in the world of work.

There are four key technology-driven trends that are already having an impact on work today and will continue to do so in the near future. Some of these, such as automation, are driving the changes, while others relate to how we are already adapting:

1. Automation and artificial intelligence.
2. The gig economy.
3. The reinvention of learning.
4. Shifts in policy as we adjust to new technologies.

Let's take a look at each of these four key technology-driven trends in turn.

Automation and artificial intelligence

Automation is not new in our lives. Many of the small miracles of modern life that we take for granted are only made possible by automation. What is new is the speed, scale and capability of the new forms of automation that are coming our way. The rate of change has moved from incremental to exponential as a result of the speed of the growth in computer power.

It was Intel founder Gordon Moore who observed in the 1960s and 1970s, in what became known as Moore's Law, that computer power was doubling every two years. Later estimates reduced that time to as little as 18 months—meaning that a computer made today is likely to be over one hundred times more powerful than one made a decade ago.

While some expect this rate to slow as we reach the physical limits of what we can do with a silicon chip, others are experimenting with new approaches to computer construction, such as 3-D stacking and working with DNA to create biological computers. These developments continue to push the boundaries of computing speed and power. But already we have at our command some seriously fast computing.

It was back in 1997 that IBM's supercomputer Deep Blue made history by beating the reigning world chess champion, Garry Kasparov. Its successor Watson won the US quiz show *Jeopardy* in 2011. Since that time, the gains in this space have been huge.

Today's computers are extremely good at analysing vast amounts of data, recognising patterns and managing repetitive tasks. This has given rise to a new group of industries and jobs focused on 'big data'—millions of pieces of information stored in massive databases. Cloud computing, which involves large computer banks connected via the internet and operated by suppliers such as Amazon, supports large-scale processing activities. Computers are now able to identify growth in cancer cells on X-rays with a greater level of accuracy than human medical staff. They can process in minutes millions of facial recognition routines for security forces, a job that no human could ever hope to do.

> **Robots are able to work 24 hours a day, seven days a week without a break—and there are more and more jobs they will be able to do. The implications are huge.**

Computer processing power combined with more sophisticated engineering and manufacturing processes has brought to life the age of robots. Robots are able to work 24 hours a day, seven days a week without a break—and there are more and more jobs they will be able to do. The implications are huge. Business intelligence company CB Insights predicts that ten million jobs in the US are under threat of automation within the next ten years.[1]

We already have robot vacuum cleaners, bricklayers and 3-D printers that print whole houses. It is clear that many manual human jobs will eventually be carried out by robots. Increasingly, computer programs will also be able to deliver elements of white-collar, middle-class jobs efficiently. We will be seeing more robot doctors, lawyers and accountants in the future.

Automation is profitable as it makes production processes more efficient by cutting out human error and downtime. The McKinsey Global Institute estimates that these efficiencies could raise productivity growth globally by 0.8 to 1.4 per cent annually.[2]

It is already happening. In 2016 Foxconn, the largest contract manufacturer of iPhones, replaced 60,000 workers in China with industrial robots called 'Foxbots', which can reportedly perform up to twenty common manufacturing tasks. China is increasingly becoming a leader in automation and big data, aiming to overtake the US in the next ten years.[3]

AI and machine learning

Automation has always replaced menial and manual tasks, but it is now poised to wipe out whole areas of work, with the increasing sophistication of robotics combined with artificial intelligence (AI). This provides the ability for machines to 'learn' and improve the way they are programmed to do tasks.

The 'Turing Test', invented by computer pioneer Alan Turing in the 1950s, has been credited with inspiring the idea of artificial intelligence—when a computer can think and act for itself. A computer passes the test if it can successfully fool a human into thinking it, too, is human. In 2014 a chatbot—a computer program named Eugene Goostman that imitated a thirteen-year-old Ukrainian boy—was declared successful when it convinced a third of the judges at a Royal Society contest that it was human.

Mitsuku, who appears to be an eighteen-year-old girl from Leeds, England, has three times won the Loebner Prize, the annual award for the most lifelike chatbot. She effortlessly carries out conversations about food and pop music, and even tells jokes. In October 2017 Sophia, a Hong Kong-developed robot, became the first of its kind to be granted citizenship—by Saudi Arabia.

Big data enables huge amounts of information to be processed quickly. Artificial intelligence enables computers to interact with us as if they were humans. While automation enables a task to be repeated perfectly a thousand times, AI offers the opportunity to repeat, learn and improve.

In October 2017 Sophia, a Hong Kong-developed robot, became the first of its kind to be granted citizenship—by Saudi Arabia.

Today we barely think about the fact that a computer is analysing our social media activity and delivering to our Facebook and Twitter feeds content designed to match our tastes and behaviours. The secret is in the intelligent algorithms—super-fast programs that analyse data and find additional insights and opportunities for action without specific instructions. Algorithms used to have to be written and programmed by humans—for example, the PageRank algorithm that was the original reason for Google's global success. Now the increase in computer power means that they are able to develop their own algorithms. In what is called 'machine learning', the computer can see connections for itself and make its own judgement on the next logical step to take to improve the efficiency of its processing.

The rush to reap the benefits of artificial intelligence is well under way. A 2017 survey by global consultancy Deloitte found that 41 per cent of 10,400 businesses across 140 countries have either fully implemented or made significant process in adopting AI technologies, and another 35 per cent report pilot programmes.[4]

One area in which there is currently a large amount of AI interest and activity is transportation, where companies are experimenting with driverless cars, trucks and even trains. Studies have indicated that computers are theoretically better drivers than most humans, and that big reductions in road tolls may be achieved by introducing autonomous cars. Many car manufacturers are now racing to commercialise this technology, including Tesla and Auckland's own Ohmio Automation.[5]

These developments raise complex legal and ethical issues, however, which will need to be resolved. For example, if a driverless car is forced to make a choice between hitting a child and hitting an adult what should the computer be expected to do? While we have already shared a lot of our personal information and preferences in exchange for more tailored technology and services, to what degree are we willing to let AI-powered cars, refrigerators and a host of future internet-connected machines freely exchange sensitive data about us?

Sometimes enhanced computing power can have unexpected and unpredictable employment consequences. The authors of the book *Exponential Organizations* tell of an entrepreneur who noticed that Buenos Aires car-wash operators had seen their revenues drop by half over the previous decade. There were no fewer cars, no more car washes, and no new water conservation measures. Instead, it was found that computer-enhanced weather forecasts had become 50 per cent more accurate, and people skip a car wash when they know it's going to rain.[6]

The battle to stay ahead

In his influential book *The Innovator's Dilemma*, Clayton Christensen explains how large companies can overlook emerging disruptive technologies until they become more attractive and profitable. Eventually these new technologies overtake the older ones in satisfying market demand with lower costs, and companies that have not invested in the disruptive technology are left behind.[7]

In the battle to stay relevant and maintain their dominance the world's top technology companies—such as Amazon, Apple, Facebook, Google and Microsoft—are all filing large numbers of patents relating to the application of artificial intelligence. Industry commentator CB Insights reports that Google is the most active, working on artificial intelligence for robotics, computer vision, autonomy for both cars and drones, cloud computing and data storage, mobile devices, wearable technologies, augmented and virtual reality, and smart home devices. Amazon is focused on logistics, Facebook on cybersecurity, Apple is moving into healthcare, while Microsoft is enhancing its software and hardware devices.[8]

Automation has already dramatically changed the face of the travel industry, with websites that scour the internet for the best airfares and accommodation deals. This has led to the emergence of concepts such as Airbnb, which connects travellers with owners who want to rent their properties short term. Now artificial intelligence is being used in applications such as Lola and Mezi, AI-powered booking and concierge services for frequent travellers.

Closer to home, Air New Zealand is reported to be trialling a new team member in the form of Sophie, a digital human created by Auckland company Soul Machines who is able to answer tourists' questions about New Zealand and the airline's products and services. Soul Machines uses AI technologies to create digital online avatars that can recognise human emotions through our facial micro-expressions and respond accordingly.[9]

The finance industry is another sector that is already undergoing major changes. The New Zealand-designed accounting package Xero is revolutionising this field, removing repetitive human tasks and providing low-cost solutions for businesses. This is part of the continuing trend of computerisation affecting higher levels of professional skills and occupations. The Inland Revenue Department is investing heavily in replacing its ageing computer system with new, automated processes. The anticipated result: a reduction of 2000 jobs by 2021.

Digital disruption is also being discussed in the country's boardrooms. In 2017, only 30 per cent of company directors thought their boards had the capability to lead the digital future of their organisation, down from 35 per cent in 2016. They are also concerned about issues such as cybersecurity and how best to use big data to drive performance and achieve their strategic objectives.[10]

Positives as well as negatives

This is not all a one-way street. While there are some industry sectors and specific jobs that it would be foolish to invest in over the long term, there are others that are growing and have long-term potential. The rise of automation, big data and other digitally enabled work will lead to the creation of new roles and opportunities. In 2013 the US Department of Labor forecast that 65 per cent of children currently at school would eventually be employed in jobs that had yet to be created.

The World Economic Forum expects that, while there will be major reductions in office and administrative jobs, and in the manufacturing and production, construction and extraction sectors, there will be growth in the areas of business and financial operations, management, and computing, mathematics and engineering.[11]

As Microsoft Chief Executive Officer Satya Nadella commented in 2016, 'The beauty of machines and humans working in tandem gets lost in the discussion about whether AI is a good thing or a bad thing.'[12]

Interestingly, research has shown that, when it comes to the future of artificial intelligence, the predictions of experts are just as likely to be wrong as those made by lay people.[13] This is a fast-developing area, and one we all need to engage with and try to understand. Whatever field of work you are currently in, or aspire to, you should assume that technology is going to change what you do sooner rather than later.

The gig economy

The second disruptive trend in the workplace is the emergence of flexible, mobile jobs and careers, the so-called 'gig economy'.

The idea of the job for life is long gone, and the concept of job security is disappearing as employers face unrelenting change and have to continually adjust their workforces to remain viable. While some workers see this as threatening, others are welcoming the opportunity to introduce more flexibility and variety into their careers.

We are fast becoming a 24-hour, always-on society. The traditional 'nine to five' job is increasingly being replaced with options such as contracting, project work, or a 'portfolio career', where multiple income streams are generated by different activities. While these ways of working were formerly reserved for those who were brave enough to take a big risk and leave the traditional system, we now all know people who work part-time, or in more than one job.

There are a number of drivers behind this trend. The first is a reversal of the traditional wisdom that in business big is beautiful, because it offers economies of scale and market dominance. Today, big means being slow to move and adapt to the times. As the authors of *Exponential Organizations* write, 'For any company today, having a permanent, full-time workforce is fraught with growing peril as employees fail to keep their skills up to date, resulting in personnel in need of greater management. In our fast-changing global and Internet-driven marketplace, increasingly desperate organizations are turning to external and temporary workforces to fill their expertise gaps.'[14]

> As the number of contractors and freelancers has increased, so have the digital tools and locations that enable employers to find and harness their skills.

The second driver is the fact that it is much easier to locate and activate a temporary workforce. As the number of contractors and freelancers has increased, so have the digital tools and locations that enable employers to find and harness their skills. Gigwalk puts you in touch with a virtual workforce. Upwork gives you access to thousands of freelancers who will bid for your project. TaskRabbit in the US and Goodnest in New

Zealand connect you to people who provide home services in your local neighbourhood. As recruitment experts Hays note, 'The greater flexibility afforded to employers and workers and the proliferation of mobile broadband are driving innovative work patterns, making it easier than ever for businesses and workers to interact, regardless of location.'[15]

Another factor is the ageing populations in developed countries, many of whom still want to work. Research by New Zealand's Commission for Financial Capability shows that most Kiwis are willing and able to work past the age of 65, the 'official' retirement age. The gig economy offers opportunities to enjoy continued part-time and flexible employment.

According to Hays, the number of freelance, contract, temporary or on-call jobs in the US has grown to 15 per cent of all workers in the last decade. In Europe, freelance roles have grown four times faster than total employment.[16]

As demand for flexible workers has grown, so has supply. The McKinsey Global Institute estimates that between 20 and 30 per cent of the working population in the US and Europe is in the gig economy. The institute defines four categories of independent workers:

1. Free agents—who actively choose independent work and derive their primary income from it.
2. Casual earners—who use independent work for supplemental income and do so by choice.
3. Reluctant—who make their primary living from independent work but would prefer traditional jobs.
4. Financially strapped—who do supplemental independent work out of necessity.

Over 70 per cent of independent workers are in the first two groups, making an active choice to work flexibly.[17]

The UK Office of National Statistics reports that in the United Kingdom alone the gig economy has over five million workers and is projected to increase its worth from an estimated £0.4 billion in 2015 to £9 billion by 2025. We see the same trends in our own region. The Australian Industry Group reports that 32 per cent of the Australian workforce freelanced during 2014 and 2015.[18] More than 300,000 New Zealanders are self-employed, a 29 per cent increase on a decade ago.

Accompanying the rise of the mobile worker we see corresponding changes in workplaces and work habits. Shared workspaces like BizDojo and innovation precincts such as GridAKL have office and meeting rooms to rent by the month or even by the hour—all supplied with great coffee, fast broadband and modern decor. In response, corporates and other traditional employers are modernising their work environments to attract and retain highly mobile skilled workers.

Flexibility vs security

There is a downside to the flexible working lifestyle, of course. Employees trade the certainty and perceived security of a permanent job for at-risk work and financial unpredictability. They may have more options, but at the same time they face a narrowing of worthwhile opportunities unless they learn to be agile and are willing to back themselves. Some employers try to gain competitive advantage with ideas such as zero-hour contracts and outsourced solutions. We all need to identify our individual appetites for risk and see where we are comfortable placing ourselves in the market.

Uber is a well-known example of a new style of company

that has few employees or physical assets. Over 1.5 million individuals around the world supply their own tools (a car) and skills (driving) to Uber in return for flexible, but at-risk, working hours. For many drivers this is a second job, or a great way to keep earning while studying for new qualifications.

> It has never been easier to try an alternative to a traditional job, due in large part to advances in technology.

This win-win arrangement may not last forever, however. Every day Uber collects huge amounts of information about travellers' preferences and geographic big data that can be analysed by artificial intelligence. What happens to those 1.5 million drivers when autonomous self-driving cars become the norm? This is not far away. In November 2017 Uber placed an order with Volvo for 24,000 autonomous cars, and the company has said it expects to see the first self-driving taxis on the streets by 2019.[19]

It has never been easier to try an alternative to a traditional job, due in large part to advances in technology. When David decided to set up his own consultancy, Creative Strategies, it took just a few days to register the company on the Companies Register website, set up an email account, update his LinkedIn profile and design a website. Even his business cards were ordered online. But despite the apparent ease with which it is possible to adopt new ways of working we are still getting to grips with what these changes to the workforce really mean. The former governor of the Reserve Bank of New Zealand, Graeme Wheeler, observed in 2017 that wage growth may be affected as employees appeared to be trading wage increases for job security.[20] Some workers are now regularly working more than 40 hours a week in a single job, or over 60 in multiple roles.

Depending on your point of view, the development of the gig economy is either an attack on the rights and wage levels of workers or a miracle of modern technology. Either way, we will be seeing many more of these kinds of 'anytime, anywhere' jobs in the future.

The reinvention of learning

Many of us don't currently possess the knowledge, skills, experience and, importantly, attitudes we need to adapt to this transformation of the workplace. To remain economically sustainable, and to make best use of the benefits of new technology, we are all going to have to get used to being lifelong learners. The good news is that the impact of this third disruptive trend, the reinvention of learning, is within our control. It is up to each of us to take ownership of our learning.

The World Economic Forum has noted, 'We stand on the brink of a technological revolution that will fundamentally alter the way we live, work, and relate to one another. In its scale, scope, and complexity, the transformation will be unlike anything humankind has experienced before . . . the demand for highly skilled workers has increased while the demand for workers with less education and lower skills has decreased.'[21]

The WEF has identified some of the future skills that will be necessary for successful learners and workers. It calls them twenty-first-century skills, and they are closely related to what in the past were called 'soft skills':[22]

Foundation literacies	Competencies	Character qualities
Literacy	Critical thinking/ problem-solving	Curiosity
Numeracy	Creativity	Initiative
Scientific literacy	Communication	Persistence/grit
ICT* literacy	Collaboration	Adaptability
Financial literacy		Leadership
Cultural and civic literacy		Social and cultural awareness

*ICT = information communication technology

This thinking throws a direct challenge to the traditional education system to disrupt and reinvent itself. While the literacies may be taught at school, the competencies and qualities are developed and sharpened over a lifetime and may need to be supported by educators at many points along the way.

Sacred cows are being questioned. For example, the value of a university qualification is now under the microscope. In 2017, a hundred major companies went public in New Zealand with the message that a university degree is not the passport to success it used to be. They stated that they were happy to employ supposedly 'unqualified' staff, provided they had the 'contemporary skills that are often learnt outside formal education programmes'.[23]

Universities New Zealand responded by pointing out that having a degree still means you're likely to earn more in your lifetime, adding: 'At university, in addition to gaining professional or industry-led qualifications, you'll learn critical thinking, analytical and problem-solving skills as well as other transferable skills that will be of use throughout your career—not just your first job.'[24]

We are seeing the emergence of multiple new forms of learning and alternative qualifications. Many universities now offer MOOCs (massive open online courses) that deliver tertiary learning free of·charge on just about any topic you could want to study. YouTube carries thousands of hours of instructional videos, and you can learn everything from mathematics to science and economics on Khan Academy's free teaching platform. Singularity University has developed from a Silicon Valley think tank into a global movement.

Industry badges, for instance a Microsoft certificate for proficiency in a particular software package, have long been accepted as valid qualifications in the IT sector. This trend towards short, work-specific learning and micro-credentials is spreading to other sectors. The term 'NanoDegree', coined by online learning provider Udacity, describes the short, intense learning-when-you need-it philosophy that may one day make the three-year undergraduate programme redundant.[25]

In the words of the WEF: 'Current education systems ... force narrow career and expertise decisions in early youth. The divide between formal education and the labour market needs to be overcome, as learning, R&D, knowledge-sharing, retraining and innovation take place simultaneously throughout the work life cycle, regardless of the job, level or industry.'[26]

Education, which over the last two centuries has been focused on teaching content-intensive knowledge, is now required to help us learn new behaviours, ways of thinking and methods of connecting with one another. Nobody today needs to *know* the capital cities of the twenty largest countries—they just need to know *how* to find this out, and how to *apply* that information in a useful way when the opportunity arises.

The *Disruptive Technologies* report advises individuals to 'be ready to re-invest in training several times in your career and proactively pursue retraining opportunities if you find yourself in a "sunset" occupation. Seek to broaden your skill set and develop skills in areas less likely to be automated.'[27]

Learning itself is being reinvented as the nature of work evolves, and we need to actively embrace the challenge of becoming lifelong learners. This involves being curious, adaptable and open to regular changes in our work and in the skills we will require in order to succeed.

Learning itself is being reinvented as the nature of work evolves, and we need to actively embrace the challenge of becoming lifelong learners.

A 2017 BBC news story explored the idea of sharpening our skills as humans for what it called 'emotional work': 'The rising importance of emotional work is likely to affect most of us. Each of us can put effort into sharpening our emotional skills as well as our technical ones. That might mean reading an engaging book with characters you care about, taking a restorative outdoor break to increase emotional resilience, or just stopping to consider how your offhand comments are coming across to your co-workers.'[28] It may be our very humanity, our heart and our ability to empathise, that drives the emergence of new work that cannot be achieved by the most precise of machines.

In January 2017 Thomas Friedman, the celebrated author of *The World Is Flat*, interviewed Dov Seidman, CEO of LRN, which advises companies on how to build ethical cultures, for the *New York Times*. They explored the need for jobs that require 'stempathy'—combining STEM (science, technology, engineering, maths) skills with human empathy. For example, a doctor may need the skills to both extract the best diagnosis from an AI computer and then to relate that diagnosis to the patient in the best way.[29]

Across the Tasman the Foundation for Young Australians has called for a complete rethink of education: a nation-building education strategy to redesign the learning system and curriculum from preschool through higher education and beyond. The foundation has identified the need for what it calls 'New Work Smarts'—smart learning, smart thinking and smart doing.[30]

> **New Zealand was ranked first out of 35 countries, because we are embracing the opportunities of digital technology and encouraging collaboration between schools.**

There is some encouraging news for New Zealand, indicating that our education system is responding to the challenge. Recently the Worldwide Educating for the Future Index was created by the Economist Intelligence Unit (EIU) to measure the extent to which education systems are adapting to meet the changing needs of our world. New Zealand was ranked first out of 35 countries, because we are embracing the opportunities of digital technology and encouraging collaboration between schools.[31]

A number of interesting innovations are emerging in the New Zealand education sector. These include The Mind Lab by Unitec, which develops STEM learning and digital skills in both pupils and teachers; 21C SkillsLab, which works to develop twenty-first-century skills in young people, and a number of universities and polytechnics that are working hard to increase their connections with industry and digital futures.

Shifts in policy

Many people, including futurists, academics and policy analysts, have been thinking about the implications of the changes in technology and the labour market, and how they will affect society. What will it mean for our country if the predictions are correct and large numbers of people lose their jobs and their ability to earn a living?

In 2017 the Pew Research Center, an American 'fact tank', asked 4000 Americans what they thought would be the impact of technology on them personally.[32] Most were apprehensive: 72 per cent were worried about robots or computers that could do their job, while 76 per cent expected that income inequality would grow if robots and computers started taking over jobs. A similar number (75 per cent) predicted that new jobs would not be created for those who lost them. Nearly all of those interviewed (85 per cent) wanted policies that limit the use of technology to specific situations, such as taking over dirty or dangerous work, and expected humans to remain in control of work processes.

Of those surveyed, 60 per cent were in favour of a guaranteed income for everyone to ensure that all had enough to live on. This concept, often called a universal basic income (UBI), was being debated long before the term AI started bouncing around LinkedIn. The subject was raised again in New Zealand during the 2017 general election. The idea is that everyone receives a basic income to survive on—it is calculated at about

$1000 a month in the US. No country has fully implemented the UBI, but many have considered it. Some argue that it would eradicate poverty and make welfare systems effective, while others say there would be little incentive to work and that productivity would drop off.

Many futurists and thinkers with a deep understanding of technology advocate for a universal basic income payment, often for quite different reasons. Some are extremely optimistic and suggest that robots will take over many jobs, which will free us up for the next cultural and artistic renaissance—while robots are cleaning our houses and making our clothes, we will be able to produce works of art, supported by a basic income. Others are less optimistic and envisage that many workers will become disaffected by the loss of their jobs—guaranteeing everyone a basic income is seen as a way to stave off social unrest. One proposal for generating the income needed to finance a universal basic income is to tax robots. Because automation will lead to increased efficiency, it will be economic for businesses to pay such a tax.

Some are extremely optimistic and suggest that robots will take over many jobs, which will free us up for the next cultural and artistic renaissance.

Some suggest that, if a universal basic income were to be introduced, this would free people from the risk associated with innovating, changing their career, starting a business, and following their dreams. In future, the quality of our work lives may increase. We may choose to scale back our needs and work less, or be part of a cultural renaissance. Alternatively, a universal basic income may make little difference to what we do.

The American study showed that the people most likely to be fearful about technology are those without university qualifications. An OECD analysis of the New Zealand labour market shows that the jobs that are increasing in number are those that require high skill levels, and the diffusion of technology is likely to benefit highly skilled workers.[33] Those with few qualifications, working in low-skill jobs, are the ones with the most reason to be fearful.

Thinking ahead

As a society, we need to think hard about a range of issues, not least about how we value the contributions of all people and provide meaningful ways for everyone to be part of society. At the moment, work is one of the main ways in which we measure people's value and find meaning in our lives, but this has the potential to change.

We also need to think hard about both the opportunities and the risks posed by technologies like artificial intelligence. As noted earlier, AI technologies are becoming very effective at analysing large data sets. But examples have shown that AI is not immune to prejudice, and can be racist and sexist, and without ethical checks will build biases into its analyses.[34] The UK government has gone so far as to say that there always needs to be a human in the loop. Some have concerns that eventually algorithms that are computer-generated and self-perpetuating will control our lives.

On the other hand, perhaps AI can help with some of these difficult issues. In 2017 New Zealand saw the launch of SAM, the world's first virtual politician, who will talk to voters through Facebook Messenger, answering their questions about issues and elections. SAM founder and technology entrepreneur

Nick Gerritsen explained, 'The technology we propose would be better than traditional polling because it would be like having a continuous conversation, and it could give the "silent majority" a voice. Perhaps it's time to see whether technology can produce better results for the people than politicians.'[35]

We all need to be part of debates and discussions about the future we want, to ensure the right policies are put in place so that it actually happens.

Disrupt yourself

It is important to remember that technology is value-neutral—neither bad nor good in itself. While it is easy to drum up concerns and fears around the impact it might have upon us, it is also possible to paint a positive and hopeful future. Think *Blade Runner* v *The Jetsons*.

The fact is that change is now so rapid and exponential that we are never likely to know what may happen to our work ahead of time. But we can learn more about ourselves, and we can figure out what we want and actively pursue the life we want to live.

Our message is simple—disrupt yourself and your thinking before something else does. Don't wait for change, don't ignore it and hope it will go away. Put yourself in the driving seat. How do you do this? The first step is to know yourself.

CHAPTER 3:
KNOW YOURSELF
by David

Some people seem to have unshakeable confidence in themselves—they know just where they want to go, and how to get there. In my experience, two types of people show this enviable sense of purpose: those who are fooling themselves and ignoring what's really happening in their lives, and those who have looked deeply inside themselves and have a strong sense of who they really are. The first are heading for a fall; the second have developed an awareness that will help them achieve success throughout their lives.

During childhood, our learning is based on looking outwards and eagerly taking in every experience life has to offer us. We use all our senses and experiment with every taste, smell, colour and texture that comes our way. Adolescence brings increased uncertainty and introspection, but at this stage we are often so driven by peer pressure and the need to fit in that we have only a general sense of who we are or might become. It is when we transition into adults that self-knowledge becomes a key survival skill.

In today's rapidly changing work environment, when we are faced with more and more choices, and more uncertainty than in the past, it is critically important to understand ourselves. As a school leaver, should you go on to tertiary education? If so, what are the best subjects to study? As an experienced employee, do you have what it takes to start your own business? As an unsatisfied career professional, is it time to switch paths and retrain for something entirely different?

The choices you make will affect the rest of your life, and it is hard to make the right choices if you don't really understand who you are.

When I was growing up it was assumed that I would go to university, so I did. I enjoyed reading novels and plays, so I decided to study English literature. This led to a job in publishing and then a career as an advertising copywriter—a job I did not know existed when I was at school. In those early years each decision was made without any wider perspective or self-knowledge.

> **The choices you make will affect the rest of your life, and it is hard to make the right choices if you don't really understand who you are.**

Now when I look back I can see how each step took me in a certain direction, and that there was a large element of luck in how things turned out. In my later career, knowing and understanding myself better, I have been more deliberate in my choices.

Jo had important role models in her grandfather and great-grandfather, who both spent their lives serving the public and less well-off New Zealanders. She can now see that in building a career focused around serving the most vulnerable she is following in their footsteps, even though this was not always clear to her. In the current phase of her work life, she has deliberately built a portfolio career based on finding solutions for social problems.

Today, when many of the traditional career paths have broken down, it is not sufficient to rely on luck in the blind hope that we will stumble on to a career path that suits us. Publishing has been transformed by new technologies in recent years. Many manufacturing and manual jobs have disappeared. Why become a lawyer or an accountant when technology looks set to take away large parts of their work?

The key to making your way successfully in this changing environment is to know yourself. Only in this way will you be able to make the choices, and develop the skills, that will lead you towards the kind of work that is best suited to the type of person you are.

Understand where you've come from

So how do you do this, how do you develop a better under-standing of yourself and the things that drive you? A great place to start is with your personal history. It is completely unique to you and has shaped your opinions, your interests and your direction.

This isn't easy for everyone. Some of us prefer to look forward and find introspection uncomfortable or a waste of time. Others have parts of their lives they would rather not look back on and examine too closely. But I'm not arguing here that you should become a meditation guru or psychoanalyse yourself. I'm just suggesting that you should understand your story—what makes you *you*.

Uncover your blind spots

One thing that can get in the way of understanding ourselves is our collection of mental blind spots. The human eye has a physical blind spot, a small dot where our optic disc is. Any object passing through this will disappear for a moment, but our mind will work to fill in the blank, drawing on information we already have to patch together a picture. Our mind can work like this too, with mental blind spots that gloss over parts of our behaviour and experiences and patch together pictures of ourselves that might not be completely accurate.

Research shows that we focus on certain things that we think will make us happy, like earning more money, even though we know all the evidence says it won't. Experts fall into the trap of believing their judgement is always right and their skills amazing, even when they only make the same number of right calls as would happen if they flipped a coin. Our minds can trick us into having illusions about ourselves. Uncovering our blind spots is necessary if we are to understand ourselves better. Blind spots are not necessarily bad, they are just not obvious to us, and they can affect our thinking without our being aware of it.

One way to become more aware of your blind spots is to look back into your past and reflect on feedback you have been given—are there consistent themes that emerge? In looking back, you might also find times when you were particularly engaged and energised. Thinking about why this occurred will give you good insights into what you care about. Conversely, there will be times when you were unhappy and disengaged. Looking at these, what can you learn about yourself and what really matters to you?

All the people interviewed for this book had at some stage taken time to engage with their history and articulate their personal story. Frances Valintine, for example, always had an idea that she was a creative person and thought she was going to be an architect or a designer of some sort. When she looked back into her past she found that she came from a long line of educators, and she now continues that tradition. Thinking hard about her back story made it clear that she, like her forebears, is a person who is driven by an educational purpose.

An important point about this process of self-examination is that it is not about judging yourself—it's not about saying that this was the right or wrong thing to do. Rather, it is about honestly exploring what has happened to you and what it has meant. Looking at the patterns of your life, whether they be in your work or your personal endeavours, gives you insight into your skills and your preferences, and helps you plan better for the future.

> An important point about this process
> of self-examination is that it is not about
> judging yourself—it's not about saying that
> this was the right or wrong thing to do.

There are different ways to explore the patterns of your life and your story, so pick one that works for you. But do try it out—you will find it a refreshing exercise to step out of your busy everyday life for a few minutes, and there might be some positive surprises.

Here are a few suggestions on how to begin:

- Meet up with a friend and share the top five things that have made each of you who you are.
- Write a two-page short story that explains who you are and where you have come from.
- Paint a picture that tells your story visually.
- If you are musical, write a song (this is what I do!).
- Draw a map of your life.

You don't have to share any of this with anyone else. It is for your benefit alone.

Understand your *why*

Once you have understood your back story and where you have come from, you will be ready to move to the next stage—understanding your *why*. It is a sad fact that many people spend their working lives being miserable or at least unfulfilled because their work doesn't align with their why. They tell themselves the money is what matters, or that this is the best they have a right to expect. They miss the opportunity to find out what work is out there that is both rewarding and meaningful for them.

People who are intentional about who they are and what they stand for usually have a strong sense of their why. They have invested time in thinking about what matters to them, what they want to achieve, and how they will do it.

In his excellent TED Talk 'Start with why—how great leaders inspire action', Simon Sinek explains the importance of finding your why: 'If you don't know why you do what you do, and people respond to why you do what you do, then how will you ever get people to vote for you, or buy something from you, or, more importantly, be loyal and want to be a part of what it is that you do? The goal is not just to sell to people who need what you have; the goal is to sell to people who believe what you believe.'

Understanding your why is about articulating your personal drivers: your goals, your hopes and desires, and the things that give you energy and forward momentum. Only sometimes are these directly connected to work ('I was born to be an accountant!') but once you identify them they will give you a clear sense of direction for your future work and lead you towards more fulfilling activity.

For Selina Tusitala Marsh, clearly identifying her why and clarifying her priorities meant she could better manage the hundreds of tasks that came across her desk: 'Knowing your why is key, because it helps you streamline your energy and your focus. So I came up with my why, my top-of-the-pyramid stone: as a Pasifika poet-scholar, I use poetry to enhance lives. It's been the common element in the tasks, projects and events that give me joy, energy and purpose.

'It's been quite remarkable to consciously put that at the top of the pyramid and then deliberately filter my choices. Then when hundreds of requests come across my desk, I go straight back to that and ask: is this supporting my why? Will it enhance someone's life—including my own—if I do this?'

Often people close to you know more about your why than you do. They can see what lights you up or drains your energy, and they can be a little more objective about what's going on. This is where mentors can be really helpful in helping you find your way (see Chapter 4 for more on mentors). It's a great discussion to have with your life partner too.

Your why can change over time, as you gain more life experience. When I look back on my days in publishing and advertising it is clear I got my energy from playing with ideas, products and markets, and trying to persuade people that something was worth buying. Now, at a different stage in life, I am involved in the world of education and my motivation and activities are quite different, although some of the skills I learned earlier remain very useful.

> **Often people close to you know more about your why than you do. They can see what lights you up or drains your energy, and they can be a little more objective about what's going on.**

Jo's why has been constant: a drive to support the most vulnerable in society. However, at times she has strayed from this purpose, taking on roles that seemed like the right thing to do or what others expected of her. Not surprisingly, these roles have often not been fulfilling, nor has she excelled in them. At one stage in her career, the prevalent thinking about leadership was that it was transferable and generic—a good leader could and should be able to lead any sector or organisation. Jo was encouraged to prove her versatility as a leader by taking on a role in a different sector and not work on social policy issues. Luckily, she managed to avoid this, knowing that the reason she was effective was because social policy and the delivery of social services were her why.

Over the years Jo and I have both done many psychological tests for work and out of curiosity (for example, Myers-Briggs, Team Management Profile, Belbin, FIRO B) and these can also help you define your why. While taking none of the results too literally, I think of them like a mirror that falls and breaks into a thousand pieces—through the shattered glass I can see some reflections of the truth. These insights are useful. You may find some of these approaches helpful too, but be careful about getting hung up on the results—they are based on global studies and population averages and can't possibly take into account your own individual history and circumstances.

Know what you value

A key part of understanding your *why* is articulating your values—literally what it is that you value most. We all have values that shape us both consciously and unconsciously. Our values are learnt from our upbringing as children, where we live, our ancestors and our country, and they have been tested and refined through our interactions with others in the playground and the workplace.

We have all seen charts, and perhaps been part of discussions, about the different values of various generations. Baby Boomers (born after the Second World War, up until the mid-1960s) are stereotypically materialistic and ambitious. Gen X (born between the mid-1960s and 1980) seek balance and self-reliance, are sceptical and questioning of the status quo, and are perhaps a little angry and bitter. Millennials (born between the 1980s and 2000) need stimulus, are globally and environmentally focused, and are looking for meaningful work. While these are broad generalisations, it is clear that our values are shaped by external influences as we grow up, and each generation has different experiences of the world. Of course, our values are also strongly shaped by our individual family context, which varies from household to household.

Discovering your values can be done in a purposeful way. There are many methods, both informal and sophisticated, for exploring and articulating your values (some useful websites are listed below). Look carefully at where you spend your time and receive positive energy and you will get an immediate idea. For some, this will be health and fitness; for others, family, work, creativity or community. Whatever answer you find is the one that matters most to you.

> Discovering your values can be done in a purposeful way. There are many methods, both informal and sophisticated, for exploring and articulating your values.

Linda Clark has a very clear view of what her values are. She wants stimulation and to feel like she is making a difference. She likes a dispute where the odds are stacked against her and she is acting for a party that is either disliked or up against it. She likes working in teams and making a contribution. From these statements, you can see her values: service, fairness and standing up for the underdog. For Rachel Petero, her values drive her to serve her whānau and make an impact for indigenous women.

If you take time to look at what you really value and the result surprises you, it may be that your current focus and time are going to the wrong things. In this case you need to understand your values better, and actually live them. Our values often evolve as we get older: the drive to establish ourselves in a career and generate assets may be replaced with the drive to have a balanced life and then to give back to others.

Jo found interesting results when she worked with a group of colleagues to prioritise a list of values and make decisions about what mattered most. While these leaders were encouraged by their bosses to be entrepreneurial and risk-takers, some rated stability as their core value. Others were surprised at how important financial security was to them and how much, looking back on their careers, this had unconsciously driven their choices. Both groups were forced to re-examine their values.

There are many online resources and exercises to help you discover your values. Here are a few you might find interesting:

- The Core Values Inventory: www.hclc.info/files/Core-Values-Inventory.pdf
- Life Values Inventory: www.lifevaluesinventory.org/
- What are your values?: www.mindtools.com/pages/article/newTED_85.htm

Your personal brand

Since the beginning of time, people have placed physical marks on possessions to show that they own them. The term 'branding' comes from an ancient Scandinavian word for the burning of a proprietary mark into the skin of livestock using a hot iron. Luckily, building your personal brand is not as painful as that!

In the twentieth century, the marketing and advertising industries turned branding into a driving force of capitalism. A brand was described as all the thoughts and emotions consumers associate with a product—the brand exists in the customer's mind. One of the things that became apparent was that every company or product has some sort of brand—it's just a matter of whether or not it is actively managed. This is true for you too.

Today we live in the age of personal brands, where net-speed communication gives us all access to a global audience and a million marketplaces. Presidents of countries tweet their innermost thoughts, and 24-year-old YouTube beauty vlogger Shannon Harris (aka Shaanxo), broadcasting from her Palmerston North bedroom, is ranked by *Forbes* magazine at number five in a list of global beauty influencers.

Even if you don't aspire to be a social media superstar, whether you like it or not you too have a personal brand. It used to be called a reputation, or what people say about you when you are not in the room.

As Linda Clark says: 'If you've worked in the media, you're really familiar with your brand because people talk to you about it in a way that I was never really comfortable with. If I go into a negotiation for someone and walk into the room with my client, and look at the person on the other side—you know that they know. It doesn't really matter what they know: I don't care now—it's a long time since I was on television, so it's irrelevant. But on some level there's a response and a recognition. In the end, my brand was all about my brain, so in my work now, that's really useful.'

Any brand manager or PR person will tell you that to get a message across you need to be clear and consistent. A personal brand is the same. It is like your ongoing press release to the world. Whether we like it or not, everything we do is part of our brand: our social media, where we work and what we choose to work on, how we behave in meetings and how we talk one-to-one. If your brand is going to be authentic—and consistent and clear—it has to be based on what you care about. If you are Weet-Bix, and really care about Weet-Bix, it will be hard to portray yourself with any integrity as muesli.

Your story ➜ Your values ➜ Your personal brand

If your brand is built around your story and your values it will be authentic and credible. You won't feel as if you are 'selling' yourself, just showing others what matters most to you and how they can connect.

Michelle Dickinson has an interesting comment about her brand: 'I've had a crutch around a personal brand. Nanogirl came about because I'm petrified of public speaking. I went to a drama coach and she said, "Oh, we'll just create a character and act her out." So Nanogirl is literally my fear of public speaking out in the open, through a persona. She was great and Nanogirl became the brand, and what I realise is that my biggest weakness was out there in public and nobody knew it was my biggest weakness.'

A number of years ago I used a tool called StrengthsFinder to analyse and describe what I am good at, and the five key words that emerged (Strategic, Achiever, Maximise, Focus, Futuristic) still play an important part in how I see my personal brand and by extension the work I like to do.

Create your own tag line

There is a practical thing you can do to build your brand. It sounds simple, but in practice it can be difficult. After working out your *why*, your values and what you have to offer others, craft a simple statement about yourself. Advertisers call this a 'tag line'. It needs to be short and to capture what you are about. It may take many iterations to get it just right.

The tag line for my consultancy Creative Strategies is 'Lead. Develop. Transform.' Jo's tag line is 'Finding practical solutions to complex social issues'. Your statement might include the skills you offer and the issues you want to work on. Use this statement on your social media accounts, on your CV, and when people ask you what you do for a living. By being clear about what you stand for, you are helping to build your own brand proactively.

Fail well

Many of the people we spoke to while we were writing this book have been very successful in their careers and achieved new and interesting things. But they did not all get it right first time.

An important part of knowing yourself better is understanding what you think about failure. Fear of failure is often what holds us back from taking the next step, from backing ourselves to move in a direction our gut tells us is the right one. So, it is important that you understand and manage your approach to failure.

Fear of failure can manifest itself in a range of ways. We can consciously or unconsciously sabotage ourselves. We leave important things to the last minute, make ourselves ill with worry, get completely distracted and obsessed with other less-important tasks, and deliberately lower other people's expectations of our competence or ability to deliver.

In business, it is generally accepted that we learn more from failure than we do from success, and that a run of untroubled successes can create complacency and lead to bad decisions. In the US, you are not considered a true entrepreneur unless you have had at least one failed company. In sport, athletes know it is virtually impossible to win 100 per cent of the time. It is what they learn from their failures that helps them improve and takes them to the next victory.

> In business, it is generally accepted that we learn more from failure than we do from success, and that a run of untroubled successes can create complacency and lead to bad decisions.

So why are we as individuals so often paralysed by the idea of failure and unwilling to embrace the risks that come with all new opportunities? Research on our brain shows that we pick up negative messages most easily. Our brains show a greater surge in electrical activity when we are shown a negative image than a positive one. While this was a useful response when we were living on the plains of Africa thousands of years ago, and trying to avoid being eaten by large animals, it is not so useful today. We have a built-in bad-news radar that can drive fear and causes us to act in ways that we think will avoid failure. In part this is because our instinctive fight-or-flight reflexes encourage us to stay away from anything that looks risky. Sometimes, though, we have family members or friends who have experienced calamity and we do not want to go through a similar experience.

During her career Jo has talked with a wide range of leaders, particularly women leaders, and a common thread in all these conversations has been the fear of failure. This can manifest itself in not applying for a role (the fear of not being successful in either the application or the actual role) or not changing careers or taking different opportunities (such as starting a business or retraining). Many women spoke of their fear of being found out as a fraud or not being good enough for their current role, let alone another one. This fear is commonly called 'imposter syndrome', and such self-doubt limits many of us. Often no amount of achievement can shake our belief that we are just not good enough and will be found out soon. Both the drive to be perfect and the tendency to be hard on ourselves fuel imposter syndrome, as does the constant fear of failure.

After many years of study Jo graduated with a PhD, but she was so sure the university would come and claim her degree back from her that she kept the certificate in the top drawer of a sideboard near her front door. You will be pleased to know that she finally overcame her imposter syndrome, and the framed PhD certificate is now proudly hung in her office. While this seems extreme and slightly humorous, feeling inferior and that we will be caught out is a real driving force for many of us.

> **Often no amount of achievement can shake our belief that we are just not good enough and will be found out soon. Both the drive to be perfect and the tendency to be hard on ourselves fuel imposter syndrome, as does the constant fear of failure.**

Through working with women as a coach and being coached herself in the past Jo has found ways that can help reduce imposter syndrome. One is to go through a mental process of taking people off the pedestals we place them on. Often, we think everyone around us is more competent than we are. We have decided that they are better than us. This is usually not the case! We need to mentally take people down from the high places on which we have placed them in our minds and start engaging with them on an equal level.

Another strategy is to deeply question the evidence we use to reinforce our view of ourselves as inferior and fraudulent. When we actually look objectively at our achievements, our successes, and the feedback we have received from others, it becomes hard to defend our position that we are useless.

The other strategy Jo suggests is finding ways of being gentle on ourselves. She tries to put things into perspective and use humour. When she has mucked something up, she will ask herself, 'Did anyone die?' and then, 'How can I share this as a funny story with my running buddies?' Turning mistakes into jokes works for her, rather than dwelling on things and beating herself up as she would have done in the past.

Linda Clark takes a similar perspective: 'I suppose one of the great things about being fifty-something and not twenty-something is that you learn to ride the wave a little bit. There are these moments when you think, I'm just useless, but I've had enough of those now to think, just don't focus on that. I'm a great compartmentaliser. I just don't carry that stuff heavily.'

Neither does Michelle Dickinson: 'I still am terrified of failure, but I am willing to do it more confidently than I was before. I talk about it all the time now. I think talking about failure all the time to people just makes it part of conversation, and people now expect to hear my terrible stories from the week, and it's funny.'

When it comes to planning your working career, it is now riskier *not* to take some calculated risks. Can you realistically stay in the same job for ten years and not expect some restructure in the organisation to affect you? Can you take for granted that your customers will always want to buy what you have to sell? Standing still is a guaranteed way to fail.

When it comes to planning your working career, it is now riskier *not* to take some calculated risks.

So be prepared to fail, but fail well. What we mean by this is that you need to develop a mindset that allows you to bounce back, to learn and to move forward quickly. This is about knowing that you have to do the work, but remaining optimistic that eventually you will get the result you are looking for. As inventor Thomas Edison famously replied when a reporter asked him how it felt to fail to invent the light bulb a thousand times: 'I didn't fail a thousand times. The light bulb was an invention with a thousand steps.'

A failure is just another name for a learning opportunity. Rachel Petero says: 'I have accepted fear as my friend. It took me a long time. It's having great coaches—and different varieties of them—and just being very aware of where my blind spots were and actually the emotions that used to come up when I was in a place where fear was rowing the waka. So now I can recognise it and actually fear does drive me. The more scary it is, the more I will jump into it.'

Ways to fail well

Here are a couple of practical approaches from the world of business that you might find helpful in preparing your own approach to managing failure.

In the entrepreneurial start-up world, there's a commonly heard mantra: 'Fail fast.' Most company start-ups will eventually fail, and their owners know this. It is the high risk/high reward environment that attracts many of them in the first place. So they have a risk management approach to constantly testing and validating their products and ideas. When they find out they have got it wrong they simply 'pivot'—change direction and try the next thing. In your approach to finding the most fulfilling working life be prepared to test, experiment and, if need be, pivot.

Idea → Test → Success → Continue → Retest → Failure → Pivot → New idea → Test etc.

In fact, many employers now say this ability to try, learn and change direction is a core capability they need in all their staff. There's an entrepreneur somewhere in all of us. In his thought-provoking book about creativity, *How to Fly a Horse*, Kevin Ashton writes, 'Creation is the result of thinking like walking. Left foot, problem. Right foot, solution. Repeat until you arrive. It is not the size of your strides that determines your success but how many you take.'[1]

The second concept is about how to make the right decisions in an uncertain environment where you don't know everything that is going on—such as the changing world of work. Drawing on an idea called complexity theory, this suggests that the best way to proceed is to place a few small bets—actions with limited risk attached—and see how each plays out. Then follow the direction that mostly works. Over time you sense your way to the best, most successful place to be.

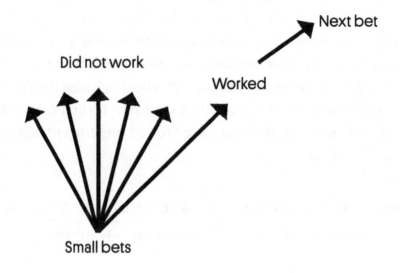

Another way to think about this is to apply a sailing analogy. Good sailors know that the shortest route between two points is rarely a straight line. The wind blows you off course and you have to tack back and forth, getting ever closer to your final destination.

This may all sound a bit abstract, so let's look at a real example. When I launched my consultancy Creative Strategies I had just been made redundant after the government decided to close down Learning Media, I had no clients, and only a three-sentence written plan for what I thought the business should achieve. I tried a few ideas and contacts that led nowhere (small bets), but kept networking and getting out and about (one thousand steps). I found some success and enjoyment in a specific area (education technology) so I worked more deeply in that space and built a highly profitable business and reputation.

Build your confidence

So failure is inevitable, and if managed properly it can actually move us forward to where we can succeed. But how do you remain optimistic and confident when times get tough?

This is one of the biggest challenges for those of us who live in Western-style democratic societies. We have celebrated and increased the rights of the individual over the interests of the group, while removing many of the supports that more traditional societies draw on to create security and confidence. Many of our institutions—banks, churches, the extended family, employers—have lost their consistency, authority and connection to our lives. We are more and more the customer in control, but with the responsibility to look after ourselves rather than rely on anyone else.

For some of us, the institutions that we work in have become increasingly impersonal. Maintaining a sense of self, and of self-confidence, can be an ongoing challenge.

Selina Tusitala Marsh: 'It's been a hard path in terms of self-belief and validating my own ideas in the academy. As a Pasifika poet-scholar these ideas, approaches and critical frameworks seem so logical, so connective, so based on what Samoans call the Va—an interrelational space between people, between people and the environment. But learning and working in an institution that educates, acculturates and assimilates others to reflect itself wears you down if you're not conscious of it and actively resisting it every day.

'Don't get me wrong, uni is full of amazing people doing amazing things too—but the institution seeks to perpetuate itself. It's taken a number of years to claim back my self—my own unique, quirky, cultural self. Now, as part of my kaupapa, I challenge other Pasifika leaders in the corporate environment not to leave their cultural selves at the corporate door—it may be the source of their greatest contribution to their workplace, to our world.'

If you have family and community that support your dreams, cherish them. But at the same time, it is necessary to work on your own resilience and confidence.

By nature, some of us are more pessimistic than others, and if we have done the work on getting to know ourselves we can identify and manage those tendencies. When it comes to putting yourself in a position where you will achieve more successful work outcomes you need to adopt a 'glass half full' attitude. There is some science behind this. When people are put into situations where they are told they will fail, they usually do. When people are told that they are expected to succeed, their performance increases and—guess what?—they succeed. This result has been found time and time again in many studies.[2]

> **Confidence can come from positive self-talk, focusing on what a successful result looks like. This is the approach that many sportspeople use to propel them to a win.**

One serious and concerning example of this is the continuing pay gap between men and women in this country. While there is evidence that old-fashioned sexism is mostly responsible, it also appears that women may rate themselves as less worthy of a promotion or pay increase than men, either through modesty, or lack of confidence, or fear of being seen as too bossy or pushy. This leads to negative results in terms of pay. There is also evidence that women look at a job description and spot the things they can't do. Men look at the description and say, 'This job's mine.'

Confidence can come from positive self-talk, focusing on what a successful result looks like. This is the approach that many sportspeople use to propel them to a win; they visualise the ball crossing the line and hear the crowd cheer. Psychologists believe there are ways such as this to trick the brain into forgetting its fear of failure.

What is your self-talk? When you wake up in the middle of the night with worries, do you have an effective process for calming yourself and focusing on happier possibilities?

I have a routine that works nearly every time. I remember the bach in the Far North where I had many happy holidays together with family and friends. I visualise in detail the walk down to the beach, the colours of the trees, the feel of the sand under my feet, the noise of the seagulls. If I am still awake when I get there, I take myself fishing!

Jo remembers when, as a brand-new public service chief executive, she walked into her first meeting with other chief executives, sat down, and found herself wondering why she was there and how she could possibly be capable enough to be in this meeting. No colleagues, staff members or stakeholders were questioning her competence, but she was. She needed to change her self-talk quickly.

Acknowledging your strengths, rather than focusing on your weaknesses, is a quick and effective way of changing your self-talk. Instead of thinking that you got that promotion because of a lucky break, focus on the years of work you did to build the skills that meant you were capable of being selected for promotion.

Write down a list of things you are proud of to remind you of your strengths. Look at the list regularly.

Confidence can also come from the people you surround yourself with. Hang out with people with whom you are happy to share your goals, and who 'fill your tank' with supportive conversation and actions. Avoid those who do the opposite. Accept compliments graciously. We are often too quick to shrug off words of encouragement and kindness.

> **Confidence can also come from the people you surround yourself with. Hang out with people with whom you are happy to share your goals, and who 'fill your tank' with supportive conversation and actions.**

Confidence is a skill that you can develop and grow. If you focus on being negative and fearful, and hold yourself back, you will not build your personal expertise in being confident. But if you are well prepared, trying hard, seeking support and being positive, you will build your confidence. Like any skill, confidence is a continuum—you can always build and improve on your confidence. Kevin Ashton again: 'Great creators know that the best step forward is often a step back—to scrutinize, analyze, and assess, to find faults and flaws, to challenge and to change. You cannot escape a maze if you only move forward. Sometimes the path ahead is behind.'[3]

At times we all lose confidence—if we are sick, when something goes wrong, if we have relationship problems—so it is something we will always have to work on. But working in conditions when things do not go right is also often when we build our confidence—our self-belief will grow because we have triumphed in the face of adversity.

Many of the people we interviewed talked about the importance of making healthy life choices, such as a good diet, sufficient sleep and regular exercise. A large part of our sense of wellbeing comes from our physical condition rather than our mental state, so it is important to look after your whole self.

Brian Steele: 'I still keep a timesheet as in my accounting days, partly so I know what I'm doing, and especially if I look back and think, how long did something take? I put a little "w" on my timesheet every day if I've walked for half an hour. It's a reminder that you do need to take time and look after your health.'

Know what you want next

Your success toolkit is now getting quite full of useful approaches. You know your story, your values and your why, you have techniques to manage failure and build confidence. So, what are you going to do with all this?

We guess you are reading this book because you are interested in your future, not just what you have right now. Time to explore what next.

'If you don't know where you're going, any road will take you there'

This is an old saying, but one that's as true today as it has ever been. You might see some interesting sights as you meander along, but equally you will miss out on some amazing opportunities.

It's very important to take ownership of your life and have a sense of direction—know what you want next. This can take many forms, and while everyone we spoke to confirmed that they had a personal vision for their future, they each expressed it in a different way, and they had different ways of measuring progress.

It's very important to take ownership of your life and have a sense of direction— know what you want next.

Some people have a written plan and look twenty years into the future. Some have operating principles that drive them in a specific direction, but they do not always know how things will play out. Others know the areas of work in which they want to operate, and are taking calculated steps to get there sooner rather than later. None of them sit around waiting for stuff to happen magically. They know that thinking ahead brings many benefits.

Things tend to go better if you have thought ahead and have a plan. Planning can help identify problems when they are in their infancy. Planning means you can spot more opportunities and be in a better place to act on them.

Frances Valintine: 'In life, for me, you have to have that end goal and that purpose of what's going to get you there. Because there are going to be days when things just feel complicated and feel like they're overwhelming. There are weeks where I literally want to draw a line through it and go, well that was not a great week, let's just bury that one. But I know next week's going to be great because I am back on track.'

Planning is hard and can be painful. Planning means stopping, taking stock, and thinking forward. If it is not something that comes easily to you, or it's not something that you have done for yourself in the past, planning will take discipline, like any new habit or activity. Thinking forward takes time. To analyse honestly where you want to go may take a lot of painful soul-searching. You will have to ask yourself some hard questions, the result of which may be that you are not where you need to be. That means either making the effort to change or ignoring that you need to change. Both can be painful.

When I sold my shares in the training company David Forman to my business partner I had no job to go to. But I did have a short written list of criteria for what my next work would involve: Leadership, Education, Technology, Growth. When the role of CEO at Learning Media came up it was quickly clear to me that this was a role that would deliver what I was looking for.

When planning the launch of my consultancy Creative Strategies, I wrote a three-sentence positioning statement that guided the growth and development of the business:

- We are a consultancy specialising in business development for the education and technology sectors.
- We offer world-class marketing strategies to build your business.
- We are important when you want to accelerate your business growth domestically or internationally.

Every year for four years the business achieved healthy growth in revenues doing just what the plan described.

If you know who you are and what you want, you are well on the road to achieving success.

Top 5 tips to know yourself

1. Understand and articulate your personal story.
2. Understand your *why* and explore your values.
3. Define and live your personal brand.
4. Fail well and build your confidence.
5. Know what you want next.

THE SYSTEM
CHANGE AGENT
VIVIEN MAIDABORN

 Vivien Maidaborn is chief executive of UNICEF NZ. She has worked in the community, disability and health sectors, including as CEO of CCS Disability Action, she is the founder of social enterprise Lifemark, and she sits on a number of boards.

Vivien has a clear sense of her life's mission: 'Capturing and really engaging in the possibilities between business, community and government for sustainable, scalable change. That's my space.'

A big breakthrough in her thinking and the direction of her work came when she took a course created by the Covey Leadership Center on 'The Seven Habits of Highly Effective People'.

'It was a complete game-changer in the way I think about my life across personal, work and renewal activity. It's much more mission-focused than time-focused, so ever since that time I've never really separated out what's meaningful in my life and my work. It brought ideas of personal renewal and organisational focus into one package, and in one way or another I've used that material throughout my career.'

Vivien became licensed to teach the Covey materials and travelled across New Zealand experiencing a wide variety of workplaces.

'I learned that it didn't matter whether I was in a freezing works or a biscuit factory or a health environment or a government department—people's organisational change questions were the same. What's my role? Are management walking their talk? Do we know where we're headed? Is all of me being engaged in that effort or am I only invited to bring this bit? Do I enjoy my team? It didn't matter where I was—I heard those questions. I saw the pride of a really fully functioning team and I also saw the devastating desert that is life if you hate your work.'

> **'We need to be thinking way more about valued roles in communities and families and workplaces than just about paid work. Because work is going to change so dramatically.'**

Working in the disability sector has helped shape Vivien's thoughts about the meaning of work.

'We need to be thinking way more about valued roles in communities and families and workplaces than just about paid work. Because work is going to change so dramatically. It just so happens that in the past many of us have found our valued role through paid employment, and of course there's been the whole tension for women in having this hugely private valued role of parenting or managing a household that hasn't really been valued publicly. People in the disability sector taught me that the outcomes people are looking for are more real and broad than just financial exchange.'

> 'There is a real movement of young people who are consciously doing the work of stepping aside from the status quo. They are being very conscious about environment, conscious about their own personal life decisions.'

Her work with Enspiral (a social enterprise that develops entrepreneurs) and Loomio (an online solution that supports a culture of inclusive decision-making) has made Vivien optimistic about how the next generation is facing the challenges.

'There is a real movement of young people who are consciously doing the work of stepping aside from the status quo. They are being very conscious about environment, conscious about their own personal life decisions. Conscious about what they eat and why in a much different way than in my own generation. Being vegan because of animal rights—not because of eczema.

'Everybody around the Loomio table has a conscious approach to their food, their consumerism, their carbon footprint, their everything. Their lives are lived so consciously. People living conscious lives are connectors—they connect to other people, to the planet and all its life forms. What an exciting idea.'

Joining UNICEF has brought with it a whole new international perspective.

'I see myself increasingly as a global citizen rather than just having a national identity, and therefore working much more globally. One of the enduring questions in my career has been about scaling change. I'm walking that line between innovation and its relationship to large organisation systems. So much innovation happens in the margins—and UNICEF is both a deeply decentralised part of the UN and bureaucratic to its core. Not necessarily an easy place to create innovation. And yet it's where scale happens. So those are the kinds of paradoxes that shape my work.'

THE INDIGENOUS ENTREPRENEUR
SHAY WRIGHT

Shay Wright (Te Rarawa) was included on the 2016 *Forbes* 30 Under 30 Asia list in the Social Entrepreneur category, which honours the most promising young leaders, daring entrepreneurs and game changers in Asia. Through the organisation that he co-founded, Te Whare Hukahuka, he is helping to rebuild local Māori economies through education and training, and by empowering community leaders with confidence and the skills needed to run world-class organisations.

Shay's story is that of an entrepreneur.

'I started my first little venture when I was six years old, selling paintings in the playground at primary school. Unfortunately, the kids didn't have any money to buy them, but the teachers took pity on me and threw me a few cents. Then I had a couple of other side hustles as I went through school, including a little design business where I designed billboards and brochures for the likes of the Department of Conservation and small charities in the Far North. I would sell succulent plants at the market. I would sell tachometers for boy-racer cars on Trade Me.'

His desire to create an alternative working lifestyle emerged at an early stage.

'My dad had a small engineering firm in Kaitaia, and what I noticed is that *he* was the business, so if you actually took him out of the business, it wouldn't generate any income. There's no difference between that and working for somebody else—that was an inferior form of doing business. What I wanted to try and do in the future was to build a system, not build myself into an income that was wholly dependent on me selling time.'

After university Shay interned at business incubator The Icehouse, writing up the stories of New Zealand's top entrepreneurs, interviewing them, and understanding their challenges and opportunities and the ways they grew their businesses. He built a relationship with CEO Andy Hamilton, pitched the idea of using Icehouse expertise and resources to help Māori organisations, and was given a free rein to set up a Māori unit. This led to the creation in 2015 of Te Whare Hukahuka with co-founder Travis O'Keefe. Together they have set some very ambitious goals.

'Our long-term vision is to improve the lives of ten million indigenous people, so it's a social mission, and we've wrapped around that a business model to enable that. By throwing such an aspirational vision out there, it's making us think differently about how we go about achieving it. If it was just to improve the lives of the 600,000 Māori living in New Zealand, then you'd go about it slightly differently. But because we have such a great number that we're trying to achieve, ten million, we have to really think differently about how we go about it.'

Money has not been plentiful in the early years. 'We've had to just make up for that by putting in twice as many hours as anyone else, because we haven't been able to afford a team. In saying that, we have consistently grown our revenues every year since we started.'

Although he considers himself an introvert, Shay has worked hard at building both the business brand and his personal brand—knowing that they go hand in hand.

'There's this marketing concept by Seth Godin which is, "Be the purple cow, or be so different that you stand out and that you are remarkable."[4] We need to be that in this space or we're just going to become part of the noise. Little things like having a bright purple brand colour in the Māori space, or wearing really casual clothes when we go in to work with Māori, so that we're not just another suit—the benefit of doing those little things has been that we have been able to be recognised, where a whole number of other Māori organisations aren't recognised.

> **Although he considers himself an introvert, Shay has worked hard at building both the business brand and his personal brand— knowing that they go hand in hand.**

'That recognition has taken us to the New Zealand Innovation Awards, to the *Forbes* 30 Under 30 lists, to Matariki awards, Young Enterprise awards, many different areas, and then just many times we've been written about or interviewed or profiled. I think this concept of "be different, be remarkable, stand out, be something worth being talked about" is actually really important as a general twenty-first-century concept. Building our brand is going to help us mobilise a community or a tribe of people who believe what we believe and who deeply care about helping bring our vision to life.'

THE CULTURAL COMMUNICATOR
HOLONA LUI

Holona Lui and his wife Trish run Catalyst Pacific, a business that helps organisations communicate effectively across cultures for high performance. Holona has also been a secondary teacher, a TV presentation and promotions director, worked at the Ministry for Pacific Island Affairs, and been coach of a number of sports teams including at national level.

Culture is key to who Holona is. 'I'm a New Zealand-born Niuean, so my cultural background has always been a part of me and it is just part of who we are. I've always felt that in my close colleagues from similar backgrounds, their potential, that hidden talent, hasn't always been tapped into.'

Holona's personal story has always been about family and community.

'Part of growing up was our parents, and especially my mother, it was about how you always give back. Our success is not just *our* success—it's actually all the people in your family and your friends who are behind that. Part of that giving back, for me, was helping people to be really good at what they did and realise their potential. So, I went into teaching to help the community, support them and other people.'

'It's important to build relationships with people, not just transactional relationships for the contracts, but enduring relationships so that the links that are built with people overseas, or in different markets, are sustainable, not just now, but into the future.'

Relationships are an important value for him.

'Roughly eighty per cent of the world is made up of very relational societies. It's important to build relationships with people, not just transactional relationships for the contracts, but enduring relationships so that the links that are built with people overseas, or in different markets, are sustainable, not just now, but into the future.'

Holona joined the Ministry of Pacific Island Affairs because he took the initiative.

'I rang them and asked if they had any vacancies, and by chance, they had a job for a communications advisor. When the job description came through I thought it was almost as if someone had written it for me. I spent almost ten years there and was lucky enough to be part of some wonderful initiatives. Some of the policies that I was part of and able to contribute to, I've seen the results of that work come through ten and more years down the track. The key has been working with those who make the policy decisions on the allocation, priority and targeting of resources.'

Starting out in their own business was a big call for Trish and Holona.

'An opportunity came up and it was either then or continue working in a job for somebody else. We had kids and a mortgage, but the kids were a bit older. They were still at home, but that was the decision that we made. Money is not the driver. It's about social influence, about making a difference to other people's lives by working with those in high-level decision-making and other leadership positions to get the best from their people whatever their background. We enjoy facilitating, we enjoy being in front of people, we enjoy working with people. We wanted work that we could take around the world with us.'

Holona knows what it feels like to take on a risk, but he has a way of dealing with the fear.

'You always wonder about putting yourself out there, taking on new things, and you think—big gulp. I always think of my mum—what would she do? She came from a small village in Niue. She lost her mum when she was six, came over here when she was sixteen, and she would just do whatever it took.'

Holona is very clear about his plans for the future.

'Our children are still on their life journey, so it's to help them do well. In big-level goals, it has been to make a difference for underprivileged groups to reach their potential. What is of concern to me is to improve the educational achievements of the whole of society, particularly those in lower socioeconomic groups. That's the goal.'

CHAPTER 4:
KNOW WHAT'S AROUND YOU
by David

When I was in my early teens I was a bookworm. I was so lost in reading stories of Greek heroes and World War II pilots that I rarely knew what was going on around me. There are numerous family photos of me on sandy beaches and beautiful mountainsides, with my head completely buried in the pages of a book.

Being lost in a good book is one of life's pleasures but being unaware of what is happening around us can be costly. Many adults are just like my teenage self, absorbed in imaginative fantasy, whether it be binge TV, online games or the flattering mirrors of social media. Instead of having our noses in a book, we are glued to a screen, or maybe more than one screen at the same time.

Why knowing what's around you matters

At times we all need to escape to *Game of Thrones* or whatever our favourite diversion happens to be. But we cannot do so at the expense of losing sight of what is happening around us. If you don't focus on the context in which you have to work, you will fail to achieve what you want or make the breakthrough you're hoping for.

An example of a Kiwi success in which total awareness of the operating environment was vital was the New Zealanders' 2017 win in the America's Cup in Bermuda. A multitude of decisions were needed for Team New Zealand to put together the winning combination of people, skills and technology. One of their most impressive and disruptive innovations was bringing in the role of the 'cyclor'—a cycling sailor—and recruiting top cyclists to join experienced sailors.

The America's Cup is famous for legal challenges, and Team New Zealand was successful because it knew in intimate detail what the complicated rules did and did not allow. It was because the team fully understood the environment they were operating within that they could push the limits of their boat and succeed. This enabled them to take a revolutionary approach, which the team and the technology took to its logical conclusion.

Contrast this with the scores of businesses that go under because they do not understand and respond to what is going on around them. Kodak, which invented the digital camera back in 1975, was put out of business by others who took up the concept. While the company initially spent billions developing the idea, it seems that they underestimated the market and got left behind. Now we all have cameras on our mobile phones, and little or no need for a separate device.

Borders took great pride in being the largest chain of bookstores in the world. But the company apparently made a number of poor decisions, including missing out on the disruptive possibility enabled by the internet. Instead it outsourced its online sales to Amazon, which turned out to be its biggest competitor.

In hindsight both these companies, Kodak and Borders, had their blinkers on, looking at the short term rather than what was coming down the line to drive them out of business. This can happen to us as individuals if we don't remain aware of what is going on around us.

Escape the echo chamber

Our minds work in ways that can make it hard for us to see what is really going on around us. We all have a tendency towards what psychologists call 'confirmation bias', the inclination to look for and remember information that confirms our beliefs. Even if we are given evidence that is unclear, we often use it to support what we already think. Psychological experiments show how people process information so that it agrees with the views they hold. We also have a tendency to remember selected facts that support our views.

> We all have a tendency towards what psychologists call 'confirmation bias', the inclination to look for and remember information that confirms our beliefs.

It's not that we are trying to deceive ourselves intentionally. Confirmation bias occurs automatically as a result of our brains taking shortcuts so that we can process large and complex amounts of information. It could be described as wishful thinking—looking for information that supports our view of the world and predicts the world we want to unfold. Think about a time when you bought a certain type of car, say a red Toyota, and then you started seeing red Toyotas everywhere. Your brain is processing information in a way that confirms your choice of car.

If the statistics are right,[1] most of us are registered on Facebook or a similar social media site—around 3.2 million New Zealanders in 2017. We spend a substantial amount of time there (on average, two hours and seven minutes each day) and we do this frequently (90 per cent of us check in at least daily). Can you wait for a train, a bus, or in a queue without checking your social media?

We know that social media sites like Facebook use algorithms to steer us towards articles and posts relating to things we are interested in. There are increasing concerns that this creates 'echo chambers', groups on social media where ideas, beliefs and information bounce about in a closed system and reinforce the importance of these ideas to those who hold them. Research from Harvard Law School has shown that echo chambers do exist in social media.[2] Data from Italian and American Facebook accounts showed that users shared their favourite stories and formed polarised groups. Confirmation bias meant that users shared posts that agreed with their views with other people who held similar views.

What this means is that it can be hard to see what others think and what is going on beyond your echo chamber. If I am a bank teller and I'm very interested in stories about bank tellers, I will look for and receive stories that confirm the importance of being a bank teller. However, what I might miss is other evidence showing that increasing automation and the development of artificial intelligence to provide customer service means that there are fewer roles for bank tellers. I might make a series of decisions based on my confirmation bias, like studying to increase my qualifications as a bank teller rather than retraining in a different field, which could have a lasting impact on my future employability.

> Educating yourself and learning new skills is the way forward. Shutting the door and hoping change will not happen isn't a sensible option.

Without a sober and objective view of what's happening out there, we can fall into some big holes. In Michelle Dickinson's role as a science communicator, she sees a lot of people shrugging off the idea that robots are going to take our jobs. Her advice is to get out of any echo chamber that reinforces the idea that the status quo will remain and to accept what is happening. Rather than denying that change is coming, or being afraid, it is important to focus on who you are, and what your strengths are, and how you could use these if a robot did replace some of what you do. Educating yourself and learning new skills is the way forward. Shutting the door and hoping change will not happen isn't a sensible option.

The reality is that no one knows exactly what the future will hold, but there are clues all around us. The following sections look at the mindset you can adopt and the activities you can engage in to become more aware of what is happening around you, and the threats, and opportunities, that might be applicable to your working life.

Be curious

As young children making sense of the world we continually ask questions—up to 300 per day, according to one British study.[3] But as we grow up, asking questions becomes less about exploring the world and more about getting the right answer. By the time we reach adulthood most of us have stopped being curious and asking questions about the world around us.

One of the growing criticisms of education systems around the world is that when children begin their school lives at around the age of five they are lively and curious, but by the time they graduate we have taught them to conform to accepted norms and not rock the boat. Perhaps that is why many successful innovators are people who dropped out of high school or university, such as Richard Branson, Bill Gates, Steve Jobs and New Zealand's own Sir Peter Jackson, who left school at sixteen.

This is not an argument against formal education, but it is an argument for reigniting the curiosity that you had as a child—exploring the world with wonder and enjoyment to see what it has to offer. The smart universities are now doing this, setting up programmes for entrepreneurs and encouraging students to explore their ideas and experiment via start-ups and social enterprises.

A survey of management and workers in sixteen industries in the US found that while 65 per cent of companies thought curiosity was essential to discover new ideas, the same percentage of workers felt they were unable to ask questions at work.[4]

The top four reasons given for why curiosity was not valued were:

1. A top-down approach to decision-making.
2. Little time for thinking creatively.
3. Safe ideas were valued over new ones.
4. Workers didn't want to stand out from the crowd.

If we are to understand the world around us and pick up on the trends that are happening, we need to be constantly curious. Successful people often describe themselves as, or act like, explorers—whether it's Selina Tusitala Marsh's exploration of the power of poetic language or Dan Khan's desire to find and help the next successful start-up.

As Dan says: 'I'm really interested in successful people, just understanding how their morning routines work, how to find either extra time or focus, or clarity to think about what's important to them. I still listen to positive, inspirational things that remind me that everything around us that has ever been built, ever happened, was built by people no smarter than me.'

If you are new to the workforce, you may have questions about how work is structured, how to apply the knowledge you learnt at school or university to your current work and how to advance. These are all good questions that should be explored. If you are in mid-career, you may be thinking about whether to change direction, other ways of working, ways of finding balance and fulfilment or advancing. If you are nearing the end of your formal working life, you may be asking what comes next, how to restructure your working day, or what new opportunities exist.

Curious people ask questions, especially about why something is done the way it is done. They will dive into the topic looking for answers. They ask questions of the people around them, seek out different perspectives and challenging ideas, and search for information. It's never been easier to find information quickly, usually at no cost. Google, YouTube and Wikipedia have democratised the world's knowledge so that we can all become instant experts. I was listening recently to a live radio quiz and the host spotted that the winning contestant was googling his answers. Rather than disqualify him as a cheat, he congratulated the winner on his skill!

Curious people sharpen their thinking skills every day. They ask questions, investigate the evidence, and find solutions. They look for problems to solve, be it at work or by doing crosswords and puzzles on the internet or brain teasers on an app. These activities stretch the mind in different ways and can make us think more critically. They ask us to look at problems from different angles and take a step back and look at what we are trying to solve. These are all useful techniques for building our curiosity.

> **Being comfortable with not getting an easy answer means that you can keep on exploring, persevering until you uncover an answer that satisfies you.**

Curious people are also comfortable being uncomfortable. Asking questions to explore something means accepting that there is often no right answer, or no answer at all. Being comfortable with ambiguity, opening the can of worms knowing full well the worms will not be going back in the can, is part of being curious. Being comfortable with not getting an easy answer means that you can keep on exploring, persevering until you uncover an answer that satisfies you.

Curiosity also involves observation. By watching what is

happening around us, we get clues about what questions to ask. Why did that happen? Why does she think that? What will happen next?

Google defines 'curious' as 'eager to know or learn something'. In other words, it is about taking charge of your own learning and putting both energy and time into finding out interesting stuff. Of course, only you can decide what is interesting to *you*—it needs to line up with your *why* and, if you have one, your plan for the future.

Ways to build your curiosity

There are many ways to build your curiosity—think about it as training your mind to be hungry for knowledge. For example, this week:

- Aim to ask five 'why' questions a day.
- Sit quietly outside during your lunch or study break and watch a group of people around you. What can you tell about them from what you are observing?
- Pick up a crossword puzzle or download a 'brain' app and set yourself goals for completing them.
- Research something you are deeply interested in. Get into the mindset of being an explorer or detective. Keep looking for layers and layers of more information. Reflect on what strategies you used, what worked well and what didn't work well. Repeat the exercise on a different topic and refine your ability to explore knowledge.
- Seek out someone who works in a different area, with different views and life experiences. Ask for their views on a topical issue.

Understand what's coming

William Gibson, the science-fiction writer sometimes described as 'the father of cyberpunk', once famously observed, 'The future is already here—it's just not very evenly distributed.'

There are clues all around us that hint at what's coming. If you invest time in finding these clues, you can use them to solve the problems you are going to encounter along your career path.

Brian Steele says: 'I think the world's going to go through a pretty exciting phase in the next ten, twenty years, and I look at people like Tony Seba[5] talking about the lowering marginal cost of certain things such as electricity and how that's going to change our environment. If you think of cars: whether we're going to drive them, whether we're going to own them. I think directionally things like that are going to change. I think it's exciting.'

> If your vision is to be a leading underwater dentist, you need to understand everything that is going on in the world of underwater dentistry: the technology, the marketplace, the trends and the competitive environment.

In the same way that athletes keep their bodies tuned for the next competitive event, aim to keep your mind and skill set sharp enough for the next challenge. If your vision is to be a leading underwater dentist, you need to understand everything that is going on in the world of underwater dentistry: the technology, the marketplace, the trends and the competitive environment. You will subscribe to subaquatic dental blogs, know who the leading thinkers are on the subject, and seek them out.

A few years ago, I became fascinated by the disruption that I saw coming into education through the introduction of digital technologies to schools. I went to conferences overseas on the topic, read books and subscribed to dozens of relevant e-newsletters. I discovered that the largest commercial education market, the US, was talking increasingly about this area as 'EdTech'. I started the Wellington EdTech Meetup, the first in the country, which introduced me to educators and technologists who were interested in the topic (see the following section, 'Build your networks', for more on Meetups). I worked with local and national government agencies to launch the first EdTech conference in New Zealand and invited overseas experts to come and share their knowledge. After a relatively short time I moved from being someone interested in the topic to being at the heart of an emerging sector. I also met a lot of interesting people along the way.

Where to find information

There are many places to find information about trends, and a range of futurists and commentators who share their thoughts on what is happening and is likely to happen in the future. Reputable publications like the *Harvard Business Review* and *Idealog* provide accessible summaries of trends and new technologies. Many companies, such as McKinsey, publish as part of their public-good programmes a range of research and analysis. Industry-specific publications may be of use as well— engineering, medical and a variety of trade publications often have articles that outline current trends and future predictions.

There are also opportunities to see technology in action.

Organisations like The Mind Lab by Unitec and universities often have open days where you can see what is happening right in front of you. TED Talks provide another accessible way of learning about trends in work and technology.

> **There are also opportunities to see technology in action. Organisations like The Mind Lab by Unitec and universities often have open days where you can see what is happening right in front of you.**

On the internet, you can find just about everyone and everything you will ever need. I made up that concept of underwater dentistry, but when I googled it I found it is a real thing, and there were a number of links relating to it. There is even a *Super Mario* episode with that title on YouTube!

Here's a step-by-step guide to help you keep on top of what's coming:

1. Write down the areas you are interested in following, e.g. the automation of banking.
2. Do an extensive online search to find interesting references on the topic.
3. Set up keyword searches in Google so you get notifications of new information posted online.
4. Identify the key online publications, blogs, videos and commentators on the subject and subscribe to their resources.
5. Check out relevant books on Amazon or the equivalent and invest some of your money in diving deep into the particular field that interests you.
6. On a weekly or monthly basis review and briefly

summarise the most interesting points about what you've seen and read—this makes the knowledge 'sticky' so you can recall it later.

7. Consider starting your own blog, LinkedIn column or Meetup to connect with other people who are interested in the topic.

Pretty soon you will be more knowledgeable than most people on the subject you are interested in.

Build your networks

One of the most powerful ways to build your knowledge and understanding is to get out and network. This is something that most New Zealanders say they hate doing. It is true that some of our cultural traits lead us to be a little reserved, and we might feel embarrassed about 'selling' ourselves. If this applies to you, it is time you looked in the mirror and told yourself to get over it.

Think of networks as providing three benefits: access to private information; access to a wide range of diverse skills and ideas; and access to influence. Personal contacts will share with you information that others do not have access to, including their expert opinions, trends, and new ideas. You, in turn, will also share private information with your networks.

As Holona Lui says: 'The networking comes secondary to the opportunity to learn. The opportunity is to go somewhere you're going to learn things, and also mix with other people who are likeminded in the sense that they are looking for growth. It's connecting with people whose company you enjoy, who you can learn from and potentially have an ongoing relationship, friendship or connection with.'

Sharing information that is not widely available is an important role of networks. They also bring you into contact with a range of people who have different views and experience, which means you will be challenged to think more broadly. Wide networks are a great way of breaking down your echo chamber. Networks also enable you to share your ideas with a range of people who can help you succeed, who have the resources and other contacts needed to get something working. Researchers have found that networks determine which ideas actually become a reality.[6]

> **Networks bring you into contact with a range of people who have different views and experience, which means you will be challenged to think more broadly.**

Jo is someone who enjoys and naturally seeks out groups of people, especially those who work in different areas from her, with different backgrounds. Her curiosity (or, she says, maybe just plain nosiness) about other people means she can usually find ways of connecting and then relating to a diverse range of people. She has found an effective way of building her networks has been to accept all opportunities to speak at events. In doing so, she is able to present her views and then, after speaking, connect with those who agree with her, those who do not agree with her, or those who want to discuss issues in more depth.

Take a lesson from those who are professionals in the learning business: school teachers and university professors regularly head out to conferences and workshops to engage with and learn from others. They understand the power of networking.

Meetups have become an increasingly popular way for people with a mutual interest to meet and come together. In New Zealand it only costs about $90 a year to set up a Meetup at www.meetup.com. If you are not quite ready to establish your own Meetup yet, go along to one that captures your interest. Just a few of the examples you can find in Auckland are the Fashion Entrepreneurs Meetup, the Korean Food, Language and Culture Meetup, and the Robotics Meetup. Throughout the country there are currently hundreds of Meetups in over 270 towns and cities, most of which are free to attend.

I started my EdTech Wellington Meetup in 2014 and it now has 709 registered members. Since my move back to Auckland it has been managed by someone else, but regular meetings are still held. Usually only between twenty and thirty people turn out for events, which is a good number for a lively discussion, and different people attend depending on the specific subject.

Many industry sectors have professional associations or advocacy groups that need volunteers to stand as committee members—a great way to meet your competitors (or future colleagues) in a safe, collaborative environment. Networking events do not need to be work-focused, however. Vivien Maidaborn says she learned a lot from joining a national learning community whose members came from all walks of life and discussed a wide range of topics. Likewise, smart small business owners value membership of connector organisations such as the local Chamber of Commerce, Rotary Club, Federation of Business and Professional Women or Toastmasters.

If you are new to networking, a good way to start can be through a passion or hobby. Rachel Petero suggests that if you love books join a book club, and maybe take a workmate or friend with you the first time. She also suggests that if the whole networking thing seems daunting start with a small meeting, such as a local branch event, rather than a large conference. Just start gently and introduce yourself to one or two people, then ask them about what they thought of the speaker or what motivated them to come.

> **If you are new to networking, a good way to start can be through a passion or hobby.**

If you don't like large crowds, you can directly approach the people who interest you. Often people are very generous with their time when you seek them out and ask for their opinions and perspective. This book is a great example of that. Twelve busy, high-achieving people agreed to give us their hard-earned insights without thought of personal reward, because they were interested in the idea of helping people to take charge of their future work lives. Write a list of who you would like to meet, and find ways to get to know them.

If you don't know who to meet in the first place, social media has made it the work of a few seconds to find out who to connect with. LinkedIn gives you professional profiles, Facebook an insight into their lives.

A 'how to' of networking

A lot has been written about the 'how to' of networking and you can search out more on the subject easily, but here is a quick summary of things that I think are important based on my personal experience.

First, go along to networking events with an attitude that any conversation is an interesting one and might lead somewhere. Be open to learning and new opportunities. Jo came to our house-warming a year ago as my partner and I were celebrating completing renovations on our apartment. Through conversations with another party-goer she made connections that led to her being appointed Chief Executive of the Book Council. Conversations can and do lead to interesting insights and opportunities.

Second, be prepared to ask questions then listen, rather than dominate the conversation. As the Greek philosopher Epictetus observed 2000 years ago, 'We have two ears and one mouth so that we can listen twice as much as we speak.' As you listen to people who perhaps have very different views or roles than those you hold, your ideas and creativity can be sparked, and confirmation biases will be challenged.

Third, be prepared to follow up on any encounters that might lead to something interesting. If you can, create a hook so there is a reason to get back in touch with someone you want to follow up with. This could be a promise to share an interesting article you mentioned, or to make an introduction to another colleague. Get their business card. Send an email acknowledgement. Have a coffee catch-up. Don't waste all the effort and time you invested to meet and connect with them in the first place.

Look for people who are natural connectors and information brokers and who have wide networks. When you connect with someone, they connect with your network and you with theirs. Some people are naturally better connected than others. By finding people who are the centre of several networks—or who bridge across many different industries—you can broaden your perspectives quickly. Brian Steele, for example, really enjoys the role of connecting people, and he will often check in with his network to find out what they are working on so he can introduce them to others.

Fourth, always remember to think about what you have to offer. Jo has wide LinkedIn networks and tries to be generous with her time and widely share what she has learnt. But she says there are only so many coffees or exchanges she can have when the person who initiated the exchange just wants information or inspiration from her.

As Rachel Taulelei puts it: 'Networking is not about accumulating business cards. You've got to know what value you offer people and what you're seeking for yourself. A lot of times there's not a match, but a lot of times there is. If you don't have the conversation, you'll never know.'

Networking has been at the heart of Michelle Dickinson's success, because it has connected her to her heroes and inspirational figures: 'My networks are crucial to me, and I'm very privileged in that I have an international network of some incredible people, like the inventor of Google Maps and Sir Richard Branson, people who have made a huge impact on the way that we do things today. Being able to network with those people, understand their journeys and their pathways, and their challenges, and also being able to gain advice from them about my current challenges, has really helped me to understand the world, from a world context.'

There is a tendency to focus our networks on people we know well and are physically close to—like our immediate colleagues, friends and neighbours. Given confirmation bias, we are also likely to naturally seek out people who think the same way as we do.

If our networks are to be valuable—in providing new information, challenging our thinking, providing access to resources and new ideas—they need to be diverse. Seek out people who are interested in the same topics but have different views, or are at different stages of their careers, or who work in completely different fields. Connecting through community groups or book clubs, for example, will bring you into contact with people you don't work with, but through them you can learn about their industries and innovations.

A useful exercise is to map your current network. Try writing down the names of all the important people in your network. These are the people you rely on for new private information, or for their specialised expertise, inspiration or help in progressing your ideas. As you write down each name, put in the next column what you can offer that person. In another column, put down who they can introduce you to and who introduced you. By doing this you will start to work out who are the natural connectors in your network.

> Connecting through community groups or book clubs, for example, will bring you into contact with people you don't work with, but through them you can learn about their industries and innovations.

Look at your finished map. Is it diverse, does it cover a range of industries, experiences, knowledge? Or is it clustered around your current work, friends and interests? Ask yourself what a great network would look like. Who do you need to connect with to build that great network? You then have a plan to get out there and get networking.

Seek advice from others

There are few ideas or experiences that no one has ever had before. Other people can save you years of learning or mis-direction by sharing with you what they know and have done. This was part of our inspiration for writing this book and sharing what we and the people we interviewed have discovered.

Research shows that people who seek advice are actually considered more competent than those who do not, especially when the task is hard and people ask for help in person.

While asking for advice or help is a sensible thing to do, most of us are reluctant to do it. Why is that? Perhaps we are afraid we will be seen as weak or incompetent, or unable to do our jobs by ourselves. Or are we worried that someone else will take over our work? Perhaps we just do not want to be indebted to someone else? Being self-sufficient and self-reliant is seen as a strength. Ironically, research shows that people who seek advice are actually considered more competent than those who do not, especially when the task is hard and people ask for help in person.[7]

In addition to networking, there are a number of other useful ways to seek out advice that will help you succeed in your life and work. A good first option is to draw on the experience of mentors.

Mentors

Mentoring usually involves a longer-term relationship, where the mentor provides advice, guidance or support to a person who is seeking career and personal development. The relationship generally goes beyond their current role, and the mentor is usually more experienced.

Mentoring relationships come in all shapes and sizes, and they can be formal and structured or brief and light touch. Many of us can name a particular teacher who made a positive difference to our lives and outlook; often that was our first mentor. Others were lucky enough to have bosses or colleagues early in their working lives who took them to one side and shared some wise words that helped them be more successful.

My first boss was an enthusiastic Welshman called Graham Roberts who became a close friend, fellow bridge-player and mentor. Graham lived life with optimism, energy and humour, and his example had a huge impact on my approach to work, and life in general. We went on to launch a business together and after three years of hard work sold it to a multinational.

Rachel Petero has been structured in her approach to mentors. For her, they have been people who have had the experience in an area that she did not have. She would actively search for a mentor and 'recruit' them, and the relationship could involve quick, informal conversations—'Look, I just need to check in . . .'—or more in-depth discussions.

When Jo was a junior analyst in the public service, a senior manager passed her in the corridor one day and told her that she should aspire to be a chief executive. The 22-year-old Jo shrugged this off, but the statement stayed with her. One of the first people to congratulate her when she gained her first chief executive appointment was that senior manager. Even small comments from people you respect can be important for your career development and aspirations.

When seeking a mentor, the first step is to think about what you need—perhaps advice about your next career moves, changing roles, developing skills—and then to think about who might be able to offer this. The next step is to ask. In the same way that you may by nature be too reticent to network effectively, you may feel awkward about asking someone to be a mentor. Don't worry, people are generally flattered and very willing to help out where they can.

> **When seeking a mentor, the first step is to think about what you need—perhaps advice about your next career moves, changing roles, developing skills—and then to think about who might be able to offer this.**

In my experience, one of the benefits of being a mentor is that you get to see the world through someone else's eyes and have the satisfaction of passing on some hard-earned wisdom. The worst that can happen when you ask is that the person will say no, and that's generally because they just don't have time.

Dan Khan: 'I've got mentors that I use, personal mentors. Like most CEOs I end up talking to, or founders of companies, it's a very lonely role, certainly in New Zealand. You've got to figure out everything yourself. You're often creating new things that didn't exist before, so you've got a lot of second-guessing when you ask yourself, how do I know this is right? You put systems in place to manage the risk as much as you can; you put people in place to help you get through those decisions.'

A formal mentoring relationship can involve a written agreement, a schedule of meetings and defined outcomes (see an example from a University of Nebraska guidebook at www.unl.edu/mentoring/MentoringWorksheet6.pdf). Some organisations offer formal mentoring schemes, such as Business Mentors New Zealand or the Institute of Directors' Mentoring for Diversity programme. A more relaxed relationship may take the shape of a coffee or lunch every few months or so. It is up to you and your mentor to decide what works best for you both.

Coaches

Another approach is to find yourself a coach. A coaching relationship is different from a mentoring relationship in a number of ways. Coaching is often more short term, with a fixed duration and a goal at the end. Coaching sessions can be quite structured, with written objectives, and are focused on particular issues, often related to performance, or perhaps an application for a new role.

Both sporting teams and individual athletes know they cannot succeed without a coach by their side, and today coaching has developed into a legitimate profession. Coaches advise people on their careers, their health, their parenting approach, their sex life and much more. Unlike mentors, who share their life experience, coaches are generally experts who work in a particular field and help you develop practical, specific plans to advance your performance in that area. Because it is a profession, most will expect to be paid for their advice.

You might be surprised by how many people these days have a personal or career coach. Jo has had the same coach for nearly a decade. Her coach knows her well and they have an open and impactful relationship. Jo knows, because she has invested in the relationship, that she will get honest, constructive feedback from someone she trusts and who wants her to succeed. Her advice is to ask around until you find a coach who is recommended by someone you trust. Many professional associations can make recommendations, and there are both individual coaches and larger coaching organisations that you will find with a quick online search.

Sponsors

Taking the relationship a stage further is the sponsor or patron. These are people who for some reason want you to succeed and are willing to invest their time, networks and even money to help you. While mentors prepare people to move up into their next role, sponsors open the doors, facilitating the move and making things happen. They put their reputation on the line to advance your career.

> Traditionally, many artists have been heavily dependent on patrons to support their work. These days, however, sponsors can also be found in other walks of life.

A 2010 study of people of both genders who held MBAs found that men were more likely than women to have powerful sponsors.[8] Women were over-mentored and under-sponsored. This will need to change if women are to be appointed to top roles.

Traditionally, many artists have been heavily dependent on patrons to support their work. These days, however, sponsors can also be found in other walks of life. For example, it can be argued that angel investors who put their money and expertise into early start-up companies are really sponsors—they have a statistically low chance of ever getting their money back. Crowdfunding websites such as Givealittle and PledgeMe also present opportunities for people to connect with sponsors.

Rachel Petero is someone who appreciates the value of sponsors: 'Sponsors will talk about you when you're not in the room. I've had them because I have a goal and they're part of maybe that wider network that can introduce you, that can talk about you. They can sponsor you into governance, into leadership, into a career, actually. But also in business they can recommend you.'

The key to attracting sponsors is doing good work that excites you, and building your skills and profile so that people take notice and want to be part of your work. It is not enough just to look for people to help you—you need to generate great work that attracts people to join you.

Boards

Often a small business might have a formal board of directors, or perhaps an advisory board whose members may or may not be paid for their expertise. The difference between the two is that a formal board has responsibilities under the Companies Act and power to direct the organisation in certain ways. An advisory board is a more informal arrangement where the business owner can access sound advice without giving up any control of their business. In the public and not-for-profit sectors you will find the equivalent in something called reference groups.

Creating an advisory board to support you individually is an idea that may be worth exploring—three or four people who come together to talk with you about what you are trying to achieve. One of the benefits for them is that they get to network with other interesting people.

Rachel Taulelei says that creating her advisory board was one of the scariest things she has done in her business, but she gets real value from the feedback and advice they give her. 'It was like being naked in a room full of people. People have this perception of what your business is and then you actually show them and they're like, "Oh, okay."'

Back yourself

Whichever of these approaches you decide to employ, it is important to bear in mind that you will only receive benefits in proportion to the effort you are willing to put in. If you do not take a coaching relationship seriously and follow through with your mutually agreed commitment, the coach will soon lose interest in you. A sponsor will not back you if they don't see you working hard to back yourself.

> If you do not take a coaching relationship seriously and follow through with your mutually agreed commitment, the coach will soon lose interest in you.

It makes sense to start slowly and build as you feel more confident that your chosen approach is working for you. As Joshua Vial notes: 'It's mostly about your work ethic, and it's about not procrastinating and not putting hard things off—jumping in and getting things done.'

To sum up, get off the couch and get out and about. There's a lot to be learnt, and many great people to meet who can help you on your way.

Top 5 tips to know what's around you

1. Be open to learning all the time.
2. Ask questions.
3. Keep track of what's happening around you, especially in the roles and industries that interest you.
4. Ask for help and advice.
5. Experiment with networking, mentors, coaches and sponsors.

THE NETWORKED
TECHNOLOGIST
MICHELLE DICKINSON

 Dr Michelle Dickinson is a nanotechnologist and science educator based at the University of Auckland, and founder of social enterprise Nanogirl Labs. Her Nanogirl science blog became a YouTube channel and has led her to numerous speaking slots at events such as TEDx. Michelle has been recognised with a number of awards for education and leadership.

Because she works in the area of technology Michelle is constantly learning in order to keep up with the play.

'Be open to trying new things and mastering them early so that you become the person that people go to when it's in the public domain. Try and look ahead all the time at what things are coming up.'

Michelle has taken the time to identify the role models she admires, and she has also put in the effort to connect with them.

'I'm inspired by those people who have worked really hard and really broken the mould. Some of them I stalked and tried to drop myself into a meeting, or I introduced myself. I've tried to put myself in the right place at the right time, so when I know that they're at an event I'll buy a ticket and hope that I can, while passing, just meet them. I make sure the one thing that I have to say is so important that they stop for another sentence. I've been quite pushy in trying to meet the people that I think could really help me.'

Michelle values networking because it brings her diverse thinking and new ideas.

'To me, human networks are the core of success in people—they're so important. And networks being diverse is really important to me—spending time with people who are very different to me. It's very easy to network with people who are like you, because you all just agree, and you're like, "Well, that was easy. We're all great." What I love is networking with people who challenge me in a kind way.'

However, she avoids traditional networking events because they just don't suit her style or personality.

'I think what's important is making sure you network in a way that is true to yourself. We have these big networking events where you're supposed to go to a place and meet all these people. I'm not that sort of person. I don't like wine with strangers, I'm not confident in that environment. I look at the people that are in my network, and most of them are introverts, and our strength is through virtual connections, by meeting online.'

Michelle uses digital media as a central way of connecting with people that she can learn from.

'Social media has been my strongest point. As an

introvert who doesn't like to put herself out there, it's very easy to do that in an online persona. Being very active on social media is a place I like to be, because I don't have to be with people—but it's also a place that has worldwide growth. A lot of my personal networks have come from online interactions. I look at when I met Sir Richard Branson: that all came about because there was an online nanotechnology thing that I'd written about, which a Silicon Valley venture capitalist read, and then realised that I was exactly what Sir Richard was looking for and connected us up physically. For me, virtual connections and a presence in the world through that have been really important.'

Digital media also helps New Zealanders overcome the tyranny of distance.

'It's really hard when you're in New Zealand to gain that bigger-picture context around the challenges. Living in a world online means that I just had a Skype with someone in my network yesterday, and they're on the other side of the world, and we're still talking as if we're meeting in a coffee shop and having those same conversations.'

'I think it should be a symbiotic relationship.
I've never just gone to a mentor and taken.
I've tried to find mentors where I felt
that I could offer something as well.'

Michelle values the wisdom that mentors can offer.

'I couldn't live without those people. Why make the same mistakes again? Somebody's made them—you don't need to learn them again. Mentors are really good for two reasons: for motivating you to hold yourself accountable to timelines and deadlines, and goals; and to make you dream bigger than you think you can. I think especially with women, we underestimate our potential and we tend not to have as much confidence. A mentor is really good at saying, "You can do this. I believe in you."'

Mentoring for Michelle is a mutually beneficial experience.

'I think it should be a symbiotic relationship. I've never just gone to a mentor and taken. I've tried to find mentors where I felt that I could offer something as well. Then it becomes less of a power relationship and more of a friendship relationship. I hope that I can keep offering things to these people, and as they grow and I grow, we grow together. I always say to people, "Make sure you're bringing something to the relationship and that you know what that is, and at some point you may find that the tables turn and you're mentoring more than you're receiving."'

THE ENQUIRING MIND
BRIAN STEELE

 Brian Steele runs Shoreline Partners, a vehicle for his portfolio career of governance roles, strategic projects and investment banking. With degrees in accountancy and English literature, he sees the world through both commercial and cultural lenses. He is an active connector of business and the community, including through Giddy Up (www.giddyup.net.nz), as well as an avid cricket player and fan.

Brian is driven by a desire to find out things, learn more about the world and try to make a difference.

'I'm a curious person, and the opportunity to meet different people and try and understand how their community works, to try and contribute where you can, is incredibly rewarding. It's also interesting where those communities overlap and hopefully you see opportunities that exist to bring those communities together at times.'

This curiosity has led him to new ventures and challenges.

'I'm not doing exactly the same work today that I

was doing sixteen years ago. I think you do have to be listening to your environment and listening to the people that you interact with, to see where things are going and to position yourself and to challenge yourself.'

He sees having an enquiring mind as a key asset for future employability.

'When you talk to employers they want people who can communicate. Some of the twenty-first-century skills identified by the World Economic Forum point to that wider ability—be that curiosity, resilience or teamwork. The people who are going to be most useful, and I think most happy, will be able to demonstrate a lot of those characteristics.'

Brian uses both digital and traditional media to keep himself stimulated and current.

'I've done a couple of MOOCs [massive open online courses] this year in the film area, just to skill myself up on an industry that I'm still learning about, which hopefully has allowed me to provide better advice. I do look at the odd TED Talk. I read, but I read more literature and history than business books.'

**Brian uses both digital and traditional media
to keep himself stimulated and current.**

Brian's lifelong love of literature supports an interest in people and community.

'I think the arts brings out empathy when you're reading and trying to put yourself in other people's shoes. Reading literature from a number of cultures and a number of continents does make you curious as to what people think and why they might think it, and how it relates to you and your upbringing and your values. I think employers are going to be looking at people who span more than one world and can bring different viewpoints, and also who can navigate their way between different worlds in an empathetic way.'

He's not a big fan of some of the elements of networking but understands its potential value.

'I don't really like talking about myself—I'd rather talk about something I love. I'm better one-on-one than in a group. In a crowded room I tend to have two long conversations rather than twenty short ones. You do need to talk to people; you often get the gold in the last two minutes.'

Brian draws on a wide informal network rather than specific mentors or coaches.

'I've been fortunate in that I haven't had formal sponsors or mentors but I've probably had an informal network of many people. You look at and then you learn from people who have done things. There are probably also mentors who are quite a lot younger than me, although I probably don't often think of them in quite those terms. With technology and the knowledge that exists within a younger community, you are learning from everybody if you're open to that. Age isn't necessarily wisdom or a one-way street depending on whether you're older or younger.'

THE START-UP MENTOR
DAN KHAN

 Originally a programmer, Dan 'co-founded' the Startup Weekend movement in New Zealand and has been a major catalyst in the development of the tech start-up community. He designed and led the Lightning Lab accelerator programme in Wellington, which mentored over 60 early-stage companies to help them achieve commercial investment. Today he's developing his own business, ZeroPoint Ventures, which exists to provide early-stage funding and coaching for software entrepreneurs.

Dan had to create a new community from scratch to achieve his vision for start-ups.

'The start-up community here fifteen years ago was nowhere near as vibrant as it is today. There were a few big investors, and they cherry-picked a lot of the start-ups to work with, and everything felt a bit elite. It felt like the timing was right to say, "How do we bring a more structural thing into the community?" which was the accelerator, something that pulls together all the mentors who are offering help.'

He's a big believer in remaining open to learning.

'My advice is just to remember all of that investment in yourself and having vision, having purpose, being able to reflect and learn and grow. That's the important stuff which will lead to all your future success. Being intellectually honest is opening up to what you don't know and then having a bit of a plan to fix it.'

Dan learned early on to be interested in how the work of others contributed to business success.

'When I was about twenty, my now business partner, but early mentor, said to me, "When you go to work in a company, don't think about it like you're going to build a career in programming. Gain your expertise, but then go spend six months working with the sales team, go spend six months working with the marketing team." Two things that I learnt from that: understanding how all the other job functions run is really important when you're building your own company, but then also, remembering that all these people doing these jobs are just like you.'

Despite working in the digital space, Dan prefers to reach out to real people for his learning and support.

'I'm very much a fan of little pieces of advice that work, rather than long things, and the TED format doesn't work for me: it's too long. I'm a big fan of using mentors and other people's advice to keep you on the straight and narrow. I also think another thing is intuition and trying to figure out what the smart way forward is.'

But he doesn't hesitate to use digital tools to track down the very best people to help him. 'When I started

Lightning Lab, my personal mentors were the people who built the biggest and most successful accelerators in Asia, the US and the UK. You've got this weird network now where it's very easy to get things done, and if you don't have the right person locally, why can't you found a company with someone who's on the other side of the world, who's still the thought leader in that space?'

He did the same thing to find mentors for the programme.

'I reached out over social media or email, and just said, "Hey, loved your presentation. We'd like you to come and talk to a couple of entrepreneurs here on the other side of the world. Are you happy to help?" Every one of them came back and said "Yes," and all of them were flattered because no one really comes to ask for help, especially when you're people who they think don't need any help because you've already got all this profile.'

Dan's a great believer in finding help upfront before you head down the wrong track. 'When you look at people, you only see the surface. You don't know how they can help, what they've done in the past, who they know, all that stuff that can seriously accelerate you and your progress and success. I say to people, "Don't just do a piece of work and then ask someone to review it. Ask for help before you do the work, while you're doing the work, at the end of the work, because you never know." You don't know what you don't know.'

CHAPTER 5:
HAVE A PLAN—AND TAKE CHANCES
by Jo

Remember the famous study in which children were offered marshmallows or other small rewards? They could have one immediately, or two if they waited. And how hard it was to wait, despite the promise of more rewards if they did so?[1] We can all be like those children and their lollies at times. We are creatures of the present, drawn to immediate gratification, despite knowing that there might be greater rewards if we wait.

This tendency has been linked to characteristics such as self-control, patience, and other skills of self-regulation that prove important to success. The four-year-olds in the marshmallow study who waited longer and got two marshmallows distracted themselves (covered their eyes, sang, or hid under the desk) or changed the way they thought about the marshmallow (imagined it was a cotton ball). These children, when reevaluated as teenagers, had achieved better academic results than their peers, were judged more mature, better able to cope with stress and more self-assured. As adults, they were less likely to develop drug problems or addictive behaviours, have conduct disorders, be overweight or get divorced.[2]

Research suggests that as we get older we do get better at delaying gratification, and this is a skill that can be learned and practised—it is like a muscle that can be developed.

Look forward and confront the future

What stops us looking forward? What keeps us focused on today and the now? There is fear involved in looking ahead. The future is by definition uncertain—no one knows what will come next. The future reminds us that we are not in control. Like the movie *Sliding Doors*, we can miss one train and our life will be quite different from how it might otherwise have been.

> If we confront the future directly and look into what is happening, we are better placed to adapt and thrive.

Looking as if we have life under control seems to be an important part of feeling like a successful adult. Psychologists say that one of the most common fears they encounter in their patients is that of losing control. If we do not manage everything, something horrible will happen. This fear leads to stress and anxiety.[3] The future is uncertain, therefore our ability to predict exactly what will happen and to manage and control it is limited. It's no wonder we would rather remain focused on the task that's in front of us now—we know what needs to be done, how we are going to achieve it and, with a degree of certainty, what will happen next.

But when we don't look forward, don't try to understand what trends are happening, what might eventuate, the future becomes even scarier. Not knowing what might happen is harder than having an idea of what could be and planning for that. When we do not understand something, or have little knowledge of it, it is natural to become worried and pessimistic. We all know that things are changing in the world of work, but we do not understand quite what, and that makes the changes more frightening. When we don't understand something, we put up barriers. If we confront the future directly and look into what is happening, we are better placed to adapt and thrive.

If you have the mindset that technology is evil, you are unlikely to be in a strong position to understand what advances are coming and how they might impact on you and your family. Frances Valintine likens attitudes to understanding technology to hearing a noise outside your house at night. If you go out and find that it is a possum, you sleep well. If you lie in bed thinking 'What on earth's that noise' your brain goes into overdrive. Frances argues that it is better to know and understand what is happening than to lie awake worrying.

So how do you start looking forward? While it can be hard to move beyond the present and look ahead, there are some easy techniques that can help you to begin.

Imagine you are a compass

Think about where you want to point yourself. Start drawing or writing down where the compass is pointing, and what you need to do to follow the compass point.

Rachel Petero uses this technique: 'I have my compass

set to where I want to go. Māori have always planned seven generations ahead. When you have that compass, you plan knowing that what you do will impact on your children's children's children.'

Create a 'vision' or 'mission' statement or slogan

This is one sentence that summarises what you want to achieve. Use it to proactively think forward, prioritise what you do now, and what you need to do next to fulfil your mission.

I was at a conference where the presenter asked us to draft a future-focused business card for our job in ten years' time. We were asked to put our name on one side, along with our future job title and tag line—that is, what we want to be known for. I wrote 'social entrepreneur' and 'finding practical solutions to complex social issues'. On the back of the card we were asked to put the three skills we offered and our mission. My mission was 'by taking small steps, together we can create an equitable world'.

Being made to do this quickly and on a small piece of paper the size of a business card forces you to think hard and clearly.

Imagine you are elderly

Picture yourself with your great-grandchildren around you. They ask you about your work life. 'What was it like in the old days at work?'

Draw, describe or write how you would answer them. What did you do in each stage of your career? What achievements are you most proud of? Including the careers you haven't had yet can help you envisage what you want from your future.

New directions

Taking some time to look forward and think about where you want to head in your career may result in changes. You may find that the path you are on isn't leading you to where you want to go. You may need to retrain, to change roles, to upskill or create new networks.

David experienced a dramatic change in his circumstances that forced him to look forward in a completely different direction. After sixteen years working around the world for a multinational company, he was planning to take up a role in its New York head office. Then 9/11 happened, and it was clear that a major re-evaluation was necessary. He reviewed his entire career path and concluded that he wanted to exit the life of an itinerant expatriate and made a commitment to stay in New Zealand.

> **Taking some time to look forward and think about where you want to head in your career may result in changes. You may find that the path you are on isn't leading you to where you want to go.**

David had no idea what he wanted to do apart from move on from the world of advertising. With the help of the well-known career advice book *What Color Is Your Parachute?*[4] he worked out the key elements he wanted in his next area of work. This led him to buy the training business David Forman—a risky step, as at that time the business had collapsed into liquidation, and one he and his business partner considered very carefully. David spent the next six years as a business owner learning about adult education, and this informed all the work he has done subsequently.

Taking that time to look forward and think about where you want to head in your career may *not* result in any changes. Your future work may be an extension or continuum of your current work. But the key is to take the time to look forward, test and then affirm—or change—your direction.

How you set your vision will also inform how you think about your future. If you set an aspirational vision, you will naturally need to stretch and push yourself to reach it. If you set a vision that takes you in a new direction, this will involve change. If you set a vision that is steady-as-you-go, this will guide your day-to-day behaviour and choices. Being honest with yourself and setting a vision that genuinely captures what you want from your life is a hard activity, but worth the investment.

Have a plan that suits you

All of the people we interviewed for this book were clear: to thrive in the future, you have to look forward and have some sort of plan. At the same time, there was a range of views about what a plan looks like, including the role of spontaneity and serendipity. A plan doesn't have to be static—being agile and open is of key importance.

However you choose to plan—be it with sticky notes, on the back of an envelope, using formal lists and spreadsheets, tossing coins or asking the universe for guidance—look around you and think forward. You will be faced with changes, new choices, and totally unexpected events. Having a plan—even if it changes often—will help you navigate the future successfully.

Like many of us, I have changed my way of planning over the decades. Throughout my early education and in my twenties I had clear goals and strived to achieve them. As a result, I achieved a range of things that would not have been possible without a clear focus, including studying at the University of Cambridge, being one of the youngest managers in the public service, and buying and renovating a house. There were setbacks, of course, and things happened that were not in 'the plan', but looking back I can see that while I was reworking my plan as circumstances changed, it was still driving my choices and behaviour.

> Throughout my early education and in my twenties I had clear goals and strived to achieve them. As a result, I achieved a range of things that would not have been possible without a clear focus.

As my thirties arrived, bringing children and more responsible leadership roles, my plan was adjusted to take account of the needs and aspirations of a wider range of people, including little people. It was hard to make things go to plan on a daily, monthly or even yearly basis. The cancer that arrived as my fortieth birthday present was definitely not in my plan, and it was several years before it was managed out of my life. That made me rethink what really mattered to me and what I really wanted to achieve—less time at the office in pointless meetings, more time caring for my health and fitness, more time with my kids. I took what some would say was a brave move, but one that made complete sense to me and my family, and stepped away from the formal career hierarchy. I still had the same driving ambition to make a contribution, so I created my own portfolio career and business focusing on the areas in which I want to contribute.

Being self-employed means applying discipline around the development of my business, so once again business planning features in my schedules for the week, month and year. But now my planning is based on finding strategies to make a difference, and identifying the relationships, positions and knowledge I need to do so.

When I started my business in 2017, I set out to help leaders achieve gender and diversity goals for their organisations and find solutions to complex organisational and policy challenges. From the start my diary was full, and I worked on a range of interesting assignments for different leaders and organisations. I ring-fenced time on Fridays for 'generative projects'—projects that I initiated on subjects that were important to me. These have included a TEDx Talk on the gender pay gap, writing this book, and research into governance in the NGO sector.

Over the first year of working this way, I refined my thinking. Rather than defining myself as a consultant, director and researcher, I have focused my portfolio around the three platforms I want to influence—gender equality, the link between literacy and poverty, and building the capability of the NGO sector. Consulting work, directorships, leadership roles and research provide the opportunities to do this, rather than being destinations in themselves. While the change in thinking might seem subtle, it refocused and re-energised me.

Having a plan allows you to focus

Without a plan, there is a risk that you will see yourself only in the present—only in your current role. As such you may not fully understand and capitalise on your skills, your passions or your potential. People who have worked in the same job or the same organisation for years often feel that they are defined by what they do, by their role and what's on their business card. As work changes, these people are going to find it hard to adjust because their identity is so ingrained in a narrow job title or company setting. With a plan in place you can look beyond your current role and think about where you want to be in the future.

> **Without a plan, there is a risk that you will see yourself only in the present—only in your current role. As such you may not fully understand and capitalise on your skills, your passions or your potential.**

Michelle Dickinson takes an *agile approach* to planning. She plans on a two- or three-year horizon. She argues that in her field, nanotechnology, change is so rapid that her planning needs to be agile. She thinks about her career plan as if she is throwing a rock in front of her—she chooses where to throw the rock and then works to jump on it.

At the beginning of her career, Michelle thought she would have one job and that would be what she would do for the rest of her life. She assumed she would get into her chosen career and 'ride the elevator to the top'. As happens to many of us, this proved incorrect. Today she is excited by the career changes she has experienced and the changes she will make in the future, because they will align with her strengths and values and will keep up to date with how things are changing.

Holona Lui takes an *aspirational approach* to planning. His planning occurs on a range of levels and incorporates all aspects of his work, life and family. He has a financial plan that is aimed at providing sufficient income for his family and helping others. He shares goals with his wider family that involve ensuring all family members do well. His 'big level' plans are about supporting underachieving groups to reach their potential, and to improve the educational achievements of the whole of society, especially lower socioeconomic groups.

'The work that I do now and I guess the work I have always done is tapping into potential, helping people realise their potential and have confidence in their own ability. I see my future work as a continuation of this.'

Deliberate self-disruption is the basis of Frances Valintine's approach. Every ten years she deliberately changes focus and direction. She is five years into the current phase of her career and is starting to think about what she will step into in five years' time.

Frances is open to the idea that making a career change may involve retraining in a completely different field: 'About five more years is the time when I really want to feel that I can step out of what I'm doing right now so I can actually take on opportunities again. I feel that at that point there'll be a next phase in my life, and it may involve going back and learning on a more in-depth level. Part of me thinks I may even totally change what I'm doing. I may get into a different field altogether.'

David has also consciously disrupted himself every few years, which has led to a globe-trotting life over the last three decades—working in London, Sydney, Jakarta, Auckland, Wellington then Auckland again. Much of this was unplanned in the sense that there was often no specific destination, but intentional in that there was a clear sense of seeking a new direction. For example, he and his wife decided they wanted to move from London to either San Francisco or Sydney and began to discuss this openly with friends and colleagues. Exactly one year later they arrived in Sydney, where David had secured a role with a multinational advertising agency.

Keep yourself open to opportunity, put yourself in places where the right connections and conversations can happen, and then act decisively to grab an opportunity when it arises.

This is a *flexible approach* to planning, where you keep yourself open to opportunity, put yourself in places where the right connections and conversations can happen, and then act decisively to grab an opportunity when it arises.

The value of goal-setting

I take a more *structured approach* to my planning. I find that constructing a formal plan works well for me, and I try to write down a timeline by which things will happen. While I am constantly open to new opportunities, I still find it useful to set goals. I have a one-page, hand-drawn plan that has an end goal in five years' time and some actions I am taking now to reach the end goal. While the path isn't clear and the actions are focused on the immediate, revisiting this page every month or so helps me focus my energies and make decisions about what to commit to and what to say no to.

While I have an aspirational end goal in mind, I break my strategy down into chunks with smaller, measureable goals. For example, I wanted to get fit and be healthier (this is the aspirational goal) and my measureable goal for 2017 was to run a half-marathon. In 2018 my aspirational goal is to stay fit and healthy, but my measurable goal has changed (I want to run

10 kilometres in less than 60 minutes). For me, having a concrete goal focuses me and keeps me honest, not only with myself but with others that I share my goals with.

Research shows that people perform better when they are committed to a goal. They focus their efforts on attaining their goals, and seek new knowledge and skills to help them succeed. Commitment is the key word here. If you set a goal that you are unlikely to reach, it can actually demotivate you, as can setting goals that you will reach easily. The ideal is 'stretch' goals that, with work, are within reach. Goals also need to be clear and measurable. It would be hard for me to work out when I have reached the goal of getting fit, but it is easy to measure if I have done a half-marathon or not. The important thing is to set yourself worthwhile goals in your plan and review your progress towards them regularly.

Changing the plan

The content and focus of your plan may change over time. A common theme from our conversations with the people we interviewed was that the early stages of their careers were more planned. Work was often a larger part of their lives, as was achieving aspirational goals. Later, as they had families and took on different responsibilities, what was in the plan or even the focus on following a career plan changed. As people grew into their chosen careers they also tended to plan less and be more open to a wide range of opportunities.

Having a direction and some sort of plan is important, but rigid adherence to the plan is not always best. Taking a detour along the way can be a good thing. When I was setting up my business I said yes to most consulting assignments, even if they did not really fit with my business plan. In doing so I gained an understanding of what was happening in different organisations and was able to experiment with different ways of working.

New opportunities will arise and road blocks emerge that are not part of your plan. This may mean experimenting, innovating, or revisiting your plan. You may still know where you are headed but you may take longer or take an unforeseen route. Having an end goal and the plan to get there helps on days when the way forward looks complicated and difficult—having a plan is like insurance, it means you are unlikely to be waylaid over the longer term.

> **New opportunities will arise and road blocks emerge that are not part of your plan. This may mean experimenting, innovating, or revisiting your plan.**

Frances Valintine thinks of her end goal as throwing a ball ahead of her to where she wants to land: 'Throw that ball as far ahead as where you want to end up and be prepared for the squiggly line to get you there—it's going to zig-zag all over the place. Taking a detour along the way is not a bad thing. Sometimes it could be something that pops up and you just need to experiment and ask, is there something in that?'

There's a lot of evidence that writing down a plan—whether to give up smoking, change your career or learn a musical instrument—means you are more likely to achieve your goal.[5] The act of written expression proves to you that the goal is meaningful and important, and that you should do something about it.

Shay Wright follows a rigorous, highly disciplined approach

to ensure he makes the best use of his time: 'At a weekly level, I am mapping out how many hours I'm spending doing what kinds of things. And at a daily level, everything is mapped into my diary. From the time I wake up till the time I go to sleep, my diary rules what I do.'

The act of written expression proves to you that the goal is meaningful and important, and that you should do something about it.

You may not go to this extreme, but at the very least I recommend you put in writing your work ambitions for the future. In some cases that might mean keeping a notebook that captures your daily thoughts. For Selina Tusitala Marsh, journaling works well. She uses Julia Cameron's creative recovery technique, 'Morning Pages', to expel the inner censor and her negative, disruptive thoughts and to capture her creativity.[6] Writing everything down in a notebook allows Selina to purge chaotic thoughts, any self-deprecating talk and any internal censoring of what she is trying to achieve. She starts her day by writing in longhand anything and everything that's on her mind. After she has written down all the noise (I need to pay that bill, write that funding application, put out the leg of lamb for dinner, finish that sequence of poems, eliminate the word 'should' from my vocab . . .), wisdom and clarity begin to surface.

Be open to opportunities

While having a plan is important, being open to opportunities is also critical. Having a plan can be really helpful when the right opportunity comes along. You can pull out your plan and check if this really is what you want, then respond quickly rather than remain uncertain about the best course of action.

My move from pure consulting to a portfolio career has opened up a range of interesting opportunities for me. My decision to take on a part-time job as chief executive of an NGO arose out of a single conversation at a party. I know what I care about, what my *why* is, and I am open to opportunities that align with that.

> Being open to making new discoveries and
> to changes that we did not predict is critical
> to thriving in the new world of work.

Serendipity—finding something without searching for it—can have significant effects. Sociologists talk about the importance of serendipity in finding unanticipated patterns in their work that lead to new theories about society.[7] We all know the stories of scientists who accidentally discovered breakthroughs. Alexander Fleming is probably the most famous—he accidentally left a Petri dish by an open window and later noticed a bacteria growth around some mould. This led him to identify penicillin. But he could only do this because he, like other scientists and researchers, was curious and open to the unexpected. He could have as easily thrown the ruined contents of the Petri dish in the bin.

Being open to making new discoveries and to changes that we did not predict is critical to thriving in the new world of work. Frances Valintine's conversations with senior managers show the importance of having an open attitude to change. One manager she spoke with started out with 500 staff, a number that over a year had reduced to 300. Of the 200 people made redundant a large number still had not found jobs a year later. The manager observed, 'The people who were let go first were people who refused to move. Their mindsets were locked and they were negative about change. They thought they had already learnt enough for their life. Their value was about what they'd already done. Those people will always be the first to go in a situation where you're automating or bringing in better systems.'

Being open allows you to see and take advantage of opportunities that you had not thought of previously. Shay Wright goes so far as to say that if we put our desires out into the universe they are more likely to become reality, but in ways we could not predict: 'I looked at different pursuits for what I would like to be remembered for—because these are the things that excited me—and one of the words I came up with was futurist. I had thought I'd like to be known as a futurist but didn't know how that would happen. Then within six months of doing that exercise, I was featured as a futurist on a national television programme.'

> Being open allows you to see and take
> advantage of opportunities that you
> had not thought of previously.

After six years of owning and running the training business David Forman, David realised he needed to disrupt himself again and find the next challenge. He sold his shares in the company to his business partner and left without a job to go to. This gave him time to be open to new opportunities and connections. Once he had decided he wanted to get back into the corporate world he began a carefully planned networking campaign to open doors. He phoned an executive search consultant, who had no relevant roles available but agreed to meet him, and then recommended him to another search firm. In this way he met with six different recruitment companies, until one of them realised he was a great candidate for the role of CEO of Learning Media.

Both David and the recruiter had to be open to explore this opportunity together. The job was in Wellington (David was then living in Auckland), the company was government-owned (he had never worked in the public sector) and it was focused on schools, a sector he had never worked with. But the change-management skills and leadership experience he offered matched the recruiter's brief, and an exciting career change was the result.

Vivien Maidaborn made a conscious decision to step out of her successful career path to tap into new technology and the energy of younger colleagues. She wanted to refresh herself and begin a new adventure: 'I felt so out of date with technology, where so much innovation was coming from; I felt like it was time. I talk about my three years of having a brain rebore. I chose to do that by setting myself up in the Enspiral collective in Wellington. I just basically worked with a bunch of mostly very young people at the beginning of their careers, finding out what was meaningful to them—most of whom had no organisational life experience. The Loomio cooperative was born in this context.'

Work hard

All the people we interviewed pointed to the role of plain hard work—both in getting them to where they are now and in what they expect will be needed to get them to where they want to go in the future. Thriving in the future will mean that you have the skills, knowledge and work patterns that are sought after. These skills and capabilities are usually acquired through hard work—formal study, learning on the job and learning off the job. Some of us will have to retrain while still working, which again is just straight hard work.

Frances Valintine talks about the personal sacrifice she had to make to retrain while working full-time: 'Sometimes people will talk about a TV show or a song or something of a particular time and I say, "I've never heard of that—what's that?" They say, "It was a cult show; how would you not know that? Eight years ago that was the TV show of the time," and I say, "No, I've never heard of it." I realised that it was because I was so immersed in what I was doing. You make these big sacrifices. It's not forever, but you need to do it.'

Time is the only thing that all of us have the same amount of. Ask yourself how intentional you are about how you spend your time and how much you fritter away without even realising. Digital devices in particular can eat up our time in unproductive ways—checking Twitter, rambling through Facebook, ogling on Pinterest. Are you consciously choosing these activities as the way you want to use your leisure time, or are you unconsciously frittering away precious hours that you could be using to develop your skills and knowledge?

Staying current and building a reputation take hard work. So do having an aspirational vision and striving towards it. Securing your financial freedom is hard work.

David's first job provides a good example of hard work paying off. After leaving university he arrived jobless in London in the middle of a deep recession and found it very hard even to get an interview. Eventually he was offered some freelance work by publisher Time-Life Books, who had a staff hiring freeze at the time. As he had nothing better to do and this looked like a great opportunity, David turned up to the office every day and tried to make himself useful.

Staying current and building a reputation take hard work. So do having an aspirational vision and striving towards it.

Over time he picked up enough skills, relationships and work projects to impress the team. He was finally offered a proper job a year after arriving! The lesson was a good one so early in his career, and that work ethic has stayed with him ever since. Putting in the hours makes a difference.

Linda Clark agrees: 'I am a great believer that actually you have to do the hard work. Some things come easier than others, but you're still going to have to do the hard yards. My future path in the law is going to come down to my ability to work hard and persevere, because that's the only way you can get good at it, and that's the only way you get better work and bigger work.'

Working hard is difficult if you are in a role that doesn't align with your values. If just going to work and getting through the day drains your energy you will not be in a strong position to explore new opportunities. It's easy to get caught in negative patterns like focusing on the weak points of your boss or the annoying behaviour of a colleague. It's possible to develop a mindset that focuses on how boring your work is or how the company doesn't appreciate your effort and skills. If your mind is filled with these thoughts, you will not have the mental or emotional bandwidth to look forward, plan and be bold.

Be bold

Some days it feels like we can take on the world and everyone in it. Other days we might be happy hiding at home in a dark room. Most of us have probably experienced these extremes of belief in ourselves and in our drive and ambition.

But to thrive in the future of work, to survive in a constantly changing environment, we need to back ourselves, back the direction we are travelling in, and back the plan we have created for ourselves. We need to take bold, confident steps. In a world characterised by change, just standing still means we may be moving backwards. Talking to the same people, having the same experiences and reading material from people with the same views as us means we are not fully understanding what is happening around us.

For me, focusing on what I want to achieve in gender equality and increased rates of literacy fires my commitment to be bolder. I draw strength from the potential to make a difference for others, and I see any contribution I may make (and the mistakes I will make on the way) in that light.

There are practical things you can do to help yourself be bold, especially on the days when hiding away seems preferable.

Surround yourself with inspiring people

Shay Wright has found that surrounding himself with other young leaders both in New Zealand and internationally allows him to benchmark himself against the achievements of others. He has found that being part of these networks drives a sense of healthy competition for him and pushes him out of his comfort zone.

Challenge your mindset about what you should do

Frances Valintine has observed that as we get older we often become more risk averse. She suggests that this could be driven by the desire for more security around our lifestyles as we age and that we think we should be slowing down.

For her, boldness means flipping this around and constantly keeping on learning, developing and trying new things. She argues that longer lifespans mean we need to keep growing and adapting, and that we need to challenge our mindsets about ageing.

'I'll probably live to be a hundred. I'm not going to retire at 65, because I couldn't afford to retire at 65. I'll probably be lucky to retire at 80. Whatever I'm going to do now is going to have to carry me a long way.'

David points out that as we get older there is actually less to risk. We know ourselves better, we understand the world and how to navigate our way through it. We may be more conscious of what could go wrong, but that simply means we need to make better plans to mitigate the risks. For David, risk and opportunity are simply two sides of the same coin.

Practise stepping out of your comfort zone

Boldness is a bit like a muscle that needs to be developed. To build our 'boldness muscles' we need to do things that are outside our comfort zones—doing this is like ripping our muscle fibres so they grow back stronger.

Sometimes we can do this spontaneously—not overthinking an action can lead us to be bold. This could be putting your hand up to take on a new project, or talking to that person that you fancy. Sometimes being bold might take a bit of planning. If you have a fear of heights, plan to take yourself to the highest observation tower you can find. Fear of the open sea? Plan a holiday that takes you there.

Do small things every day that make you uncomfortable

Once we have built our boldness muscle, we need to keep training. Doing something that makes you uncomfortable at least once a day will keep you 'bold fit'. You could speak to someone you don't know at a networking event, approach someone for a new job, ask your boss for a pay rise, stand up for someone else rather than sit back quietly watching, or try your hand at a new skill.

Picture yourself as bold

Top athletes know this trick. They visualise themselves winning the game, coming first in the race or jumping the highest bar. Try practising thinking about yourself as bold—what are you doing, saying? Where are you?

Seeing yourself as bold will help you *be* bold.

Top 5 tips for planning

1. Look forward, and confront the future.
2. Make a plan with specific goals.
3. Be open to opportunities and changing the plan.
4. Work hard and surround yourself with people who challenge your thinking.
5. Be bold and back yourself.

THE PLANNED DISRUPTER
FRANCES VALINTINE

Frances Valintine is an education futurist, and the founder and chair of The Mind Lab by Unitec and Tech Futures Lab. She has won many awards for her educational programmes and is known for her commitment to improving outcomes for students through disrupting the current education system.

Frances has a clear model and plan for her career. It involves actively disrupting herself every decade. She is currently halfway through a decade and is already thinking about her potential career in five years' time.

At present, she is driven to change the education system so that it better reflects the needs of students with respect to their futures. Her awareness of this need arose from observations she made about New Zealand's skill deficits while overseas.

'I was spending time offshore and talking to people about types of jobs, and where the gaps in the market were. People were moving into these areas. I would come back to New Zealand and realise that we had no one in education even preparing for these emerging markets. I was looking at anything from machine learning and computer vision to AI and automation, cybersecurity and data scientists.'

In thinking about what she wanted to work on and achieve, Frances realised she would need to retrain to be relevant.

'I realised I really had to think about how I could change education, so that it would reflect the future, but also take me, myself, on that same journey. I needed to reinvent myself, because at that point I was still very much a product of my time—a child of the seventies who had grown up and assumed that whatever I landed in, that would be for life. The realisation came that I had a massive use-by date on my career coming up, because even though I was comfortable with technology, my working knowledge was more at a business level.'

While working full-time with children, she undertook a Master's degree.

'At the age of forty I went back to do a Master's part-time while I was CEO of a company in Melbourne. It was at a time when I was spending almost two weeks a month offshore. I just thought, okay, I'm just going to have to challenge myself, because if I don't start learning again and commit to this, I may never do it. That was really the catalyst for me getting back into study.'

Her study led her to start The Mind Lab, which exposes teachers and students to new technology.

'It was the scariest stage of my life, because it was throwing everything I knew into the wind and really putting another gear into the gearbox. On one level, I was financially risking everything, starting a business on my own. That in itself creates huge anxiety, because suddenly you've got no income, your salary's gone, your savings are going into something that you just believe in. You're believing in it for a reason that is personal, and you're hoping like hell that actually others will see the same thing. You can talk to a lot of people, but at the end of the day, until you actually do it, you really don't know how people will react.'

Her work is varied, but informed by her personal mission.

> **'You can talk to a lot of people, but at the end of the day, until you actually do it, you really don't know how people will react.'**

'I spend a lot of time speaking with schools and working with the not-for-profit sector, and that's the bit I give back. Sitting on boards as well, particularly not-for-profit boards. I want to do good things in this country with people who perhaps don't have the financial means. It is important for me to run some of our programmes at The Mind Lab as a social enterprise. We've got all these school programmes which just break even. We have to have it so that it's a well-oiled machine, but actually it's not about profit. Then I have commercial ventures in terms of working with postgraduate students, companies and boards in digital transformation. I have a business card that's schizophrenic. It's a two-sided one, but it probably could be four-sided. I think that's again part of this new economy. You wear all these different hats and it's not just about the one that pays the money, but the one that makes the whole person.'

Frances is already thinking about the next phase in her career and how she will actively disrupt herself to achieve it, and then the next phase after that.

'By 2020, for example, in India, over half the population's going to be under the age of twenty-five. What happens when you get 650 million people who are young and rewriting the rules of the world? We're an ageing population—we're so not representative of the world. I think what I want to do is go in there and throw myself into it. Maybe it means learning in Shanghai or going into Mumbai and spending some time. I just think that will be a new catalyst for saying, what will I look like into my fifties? I imagine at sixty I'll do the same again. I really love this idea that you constantly reinvent yourself. Because the worst thing for me would be to put yourself to pasture and say to yourself, well, I've kind of done my bit.'

THE PRAGMATIC
POWERHOUSE
RACHEL TAULELEI

Rachel Taulelei (Ngāti Raukawa, Ngāti Rarua) is an award-winning entrepreneur and businesswoman who has demonstrated a strong commitment to sustainability, as well as support for the establishment and growth of other people and companies. As founder and CEO of Yellow Brick Road, Rachel has led change in the New Zealand fishing industry, developing an innovative, provenance-based supply of responsibly caught fresh premium seafood to hundreds of establishments across the country. She has taken this demonstrable commitment to kaitiakitanga—guardianship and legacy— into her current role as CEO of Māori food and beverage company Kono.

Rachel is determined and focused on her future, but in a way that acknowledges the dynamic change around her.

'Our world is so dynamic and so connected and so visible that while it is great to have personal and professional plans or ideas of where you wish to go, I think that to put them too far in the future would be—not unadvisable, because some people do love to do that—but I think there's sometimes a futility to doing that, because the world is changing too quickly. A couple of years will pass in a blink. Five years seems like quite a solid amount of time to make long-term goals. If you're ambitious and you wish to get to a certain place, you need to step that out, starting from where you need to get to and asking what it is going to take to fill the steps between here and there.'

She also draws heavily on her culture and family, and focuses on changing mindsets that might be barriers to success.

'There's a place for the kūmara not speaking of its own sweetness. Equally, I think this can be an inhibitor for young Māori in particular because I think that you have to know what's great about you. I talked to a group of Māori kids a couple of weeks ago and asked them, "What's your superpower? What makes you, *you*? What makes you a world-beater?" One of the parents said to me, "Oh, maybe they don't want to say it because that's not the kind of thing we do." I said, "This is a safe environment, you guys. If you don't know what makes you *you*, it will be really hard for anyone else to determine that. This is not about being boastful—this is just about understanding what your strength is."'

Looking back, Rachel can see that she has always been driven, but has also been open and agile with her plans.

'I thought I was going to be a doctor and even enrolled in pre-med. Then I realised that I might lack the gene. So

I shuffled left and carried on with a law degree, which was perfect, much more my style. At the end of university, I started gatecrashing a bunch of events my dad was involved with, and I was there so often they offered me a job. That was the next really fantastic chapter, because I'd spent my last five years studying ways to litigate a way around grievances, and then was introduced to business and how you can take your work to a positive space. That was again, I guess, much like shuffling from the pre-med line to the law line.'

> "If they're sitting on a train and going to work, I always encourage people to think about why they're doing what they're doing. Do they love it? Are they doing well at it? Can they do better at it? Because not everyone loves their job.'

The critical thing for Rachel is and has always been working on what she thinks is important. She shares this lesson widely with the young people she works with.

'I think they would have to think about what they love in their life. What's important to them? What are their priorities in life? And understand what makes them so, because that will tell them a lot about themselves. For most people it will be their family and this and that and the next thing—what are the commonalities between that, so they can start identifying what is important for them in their surroundings.

'I think that if they're sitting on a train and going to work, I always, always, always—it's a bit of a cliché—but I always encourage people to think about why they're doing what they're doing. Do they love it? Are they doing well at it? Can they do better at it? Because not everyone loves their job.

'I think most people *do* their job—most people don't *love* their job. But in an ideal world you've got to attach yourself to something, otherwise it's very dreary and there's a lot of drudgery. Until you really feel an attachment to something, it will just be going through the motions.'

THE EXPERIMENTAL ANALYST
JOSHUA VIAL

 Joshua Vial is an entrepreneur and programmer with a passion for business, technology and social change. He has been running technology businesses for the last dozen years and launched Enspiral in 2010. He co-founded Enspiral Dev Academy in 2013 and is currently serving as a Catalyst of the Enspiral network while launching a number of ventures.

Joshua draws deeply on his background growing up around ashrams, and early exposure to meditation and deep spirituality alongside analytical skills as a programmer. This has framed how he views his future. He has calculated how many years and months he is likely to be alive and aims to maximise his contribution.

He focuses on his current habits and how they prepare him to navigate his future.

'I don't have a long-term plan. I think more about habits. I'm not very goal oriented. There are so many times I've seen the future diverge from what I thought would happen, that I feel goals aren't useful in the long term. There is a real sense that the future I inhabit is the one I create now, but it's not going to be "I want to achieve this by that date," or "I'm going to climb that mountain" or "close that deal". It happens naturally when I get excited about something. What I focus on is much more about what I am doing every day that will support the future I want to see. Exercise, health, food, friends, work . . . all those kinds of things.'

Drawing the most out of each day in order to prepare for the future means he is always reflecting.

'I'm passionate about constant reflection and constant improvement and oh, why didn't I go to the gym that day? Learning more about how I work, so that I can set up habits which make the future as good as it can be.'

Preparing for the future is about becoming better at learning so he is able to adapt and flourish in what his future presents.

'I've grown a lot more passionate about learning and education in the last couple of years, and about just what do I learn, how do I learn it, what am I learning now and why? Then I think about investing in relationships and reputation. It's a case of, what's the game plan there, and what's the life I want to lead there? It's mostly about building finances or building skills or building assets you can leverage. That's growing capability to deploy on whatever makes sense in the future. Often I think a lot more about preparation and planning. It's about, how can I show up to whatever the future brings and have the best chance of contributing something of value?'

Joshua's view of the future of technology is that the

ability to learn will be the critical success factor.

'Technology. It's going to change fast and it's going to change the shape of the world. It already is and it will do so more. I would say become fluent in learning and actually always be learning something.'

He sees investing in relationships, in particular, as an investment in his future. He knows that it takes a team to get a good idea off the ground, and trusted relationships are key to this. He also has a plan to make his friends rich so they can invest in future projects.

'Enspiral's very consciously designed to be a place where people could meet their future co-founders. There's a lot of people in that group who I'd happily work with on very fun things, important things, and they're more likely to jump in now because of all the work I've done just helping them succeed.

'One of my favourite things at the beginning of Enspiral was that getting investment for your business is hard. The best way to do it is to have rich friends. It's not that great to go and make friends with rich people just because you want their money—that won't work very well—but if you can make all your friends rich, it doesn't matter about your own personal wealth. It matters much more about the wealth of my wider community, who can quickly swarm on things worth investing in. It turns out it takes a long time to make your friends rich, and I'm still working on it. But I think the strategy overall is a sound one.'

CHAPTER 6:
LOOK AFTER YOURSELF

by Jo

It took a big wake-up call to get me to really start to invest in my wellbeing: a tango with cancer. Following years of chemo and surgery I vowed to change how I worked so that exercise was part of my working day. I now know that I need to invest in the health and wellbeing of my body if it is going to keep up with what my mind has planned for it in the future. With a group of friends, I started a long, slow plod to fitness, walking five minutes between lamp posts and jogging one minute. A year later I lined up for my first half-marathon. I have now built running into my schedule, and it is as legitimate a diary entry as a client meeting or deadline.

Many of us probably spend more time cleaning and servicing our cars than we spend caring for our bodies. There's a range of reasons why we don't give more priority to looking after ourselves. Sometimes we are just not in tune with our bodies, and we don't realise how unhealthy we are. We may think we are invincible, and that our body and mind will always be strong, because they have been that way in the past. Or we may prioritise other things—looking after others or finishing a project before we think about looking after our bodies. Perhaps we simply lack the motivation to get off the couch and into our sneakers for that walk around the block.

Our work and our health are interrelated, and sometimes it is work that gets the upper hand. David experienced this a few years ago when he was leading a complex restructure that affected dozens of people's futures. The stress of working confidentially, every day sending highly sensitive emails and documents to board members and senior colleagues, finally manifested itself physically. His hand started shaking violently when he went to press the 'Send' button. For a couple of days, until the symptoms subsided, he had to ask his executive assistant to take over the keyboard.

Each year, work takes the ultimate fatal toll on somewhere between 600 and 900 New Zealanders. An estimated further 30,000 people develop serious but non-fatal work-related ill-health.[1] We tend to think that these people work in 'dangerous' jobs, perhaps in unsafe factories or on building sites, but in fact the impact of working long hours under stress reaches all types of workers.

And just as work impacts on our health, our health also has a direct impact on our productivity. Australian research comparing healthy and unhealthy workers found that the healthiest people were almost three times more productive than their unhealthy colleagues.[2] According to WorkSafe New Zealand, 43 per cent of us described working when we were overtired, 23 per cent made mistakes because we had been working too long without a break, and 11 per cent reported working while hung-over or under the influence of drugs.[3]

> **Looking after ourselves has always mattered.
> Looking after ourselves so we survive and
> thrive in the future of work *really* matters.**

In the changing world of work that we all face, being on top of our game physically and mentally has never been more important. Managing ourselves through change will take energy—more energy than normal. Keeping positive as we search out and take advantage of new opportunities or undertake retraining will demand healthy minds supported by healthy bodies.

Looking after ourselves has always mattered. Looking after ourselves so we survive and thrive in the future of work *really* matters.

Invest in yourself

Get fit, stay fit, eat well—every day we are bombarded with messages about how important it is to do these things. There are whole industries based around advice on how to live well. Sometimes, though, it all just seems too much of an effort in an already busy life.

Finding the time to invest in yourself might seem hard, but it's vital if you are to stay healthy and thrive as you navigate your place in the future world of work.

Let's take a look at some practical ideas for investing in yourself.

Diary your exercise

Shay Wright has found that making exercise part of his daily schedule works for him. He also uses an online tool—a wellness inventory—to help him assess how well he is doing against a series of wellbeing dimensions. This makes him consciously focus on his wellbeing, and means he puts aside time in his diary for things that keep him physically and mentally well.

I do this as well. When I set my goal of running a half-marathon I made it very public and connected with good friends who had the same goal, and I have diary entries that are blocked out for training to remind me that this is as important as all the other things in my diary.

Think about what you eat

When Michelle Dickinson realised that some foods just did not suit her, she took the time to work out what she should be eating. She credits her energy to her focus on her nutrition.

'I'm a big advocate of food and nutrition as a personal thing—the science out there that says to eat this, eat that, whatever. I have spent a lot of time figuring out what works for me, and I think it's a very individual journey. People say, "How do you have so much energy? How can you do that?" Actually, what goes into my body is really important to sustain my energy and to keep me healthy.'

Learn something new

Most of the people we interviewed actively invest in learning new things. They all see this as a way to ensure their minds stay nimble and to stretch themselves beyond their comfort zones. The act of continuously learning, and learning how to learn, is what they are investing in.

Set up rituals that generate energy

Instead of leaving your desk at 3pm to go and buy your favourite chocolate bar, set up a healthy routine that will generate energy.

Vivien Maidaborn starts her day by using a routine that sets her up to be her most productive. She knows her natural rhythm is to begin the day gently and slowly, so she will do some yoga and her meditative practice, have breakfast and feed her chooks, then cycle to work. By following this routine, she is centred, stretched and positive, and able to throw herself into work all day.

David learned long ago that he is neither a jogger nor a gym bunny. He aims to swim regularly, and after work he will often get off the bus several stops early and walk the rest of the way—every bit makes a difference. For his mental relaxation, he loses himself in writing music and playing one of his nine guitars.

Develop routines to ensure quality sleep

Poor sleeping habits affect our ability to concentrate, our moods and our reaction times. Chronic lack of sleep adversely affects our memory, reduces our immunity, and can shorten our lives. Sensible approaches include having a sleep routine: go to bed at the same time every night; avoid screens close to sleep times; get sun and exercise during the day, and don't eat and drink heavily before bed.

Being proactive is key

However you do it—whether it is travelling to experience different cultures, learning to knit, eating well, running, or creating routines that ensure you are the most effective you can be—you need to invest in mental and physical wellbeing.

The key is to be proactive. I have a Post-it note on the wall by my desk, with this saying on it: 'How we spend our day is, of course, how we spend our lives.' The saying is credited to a woman called Annie Dillard. I don't know who Annie is, but I do know that she is a wise woman.

However you do it—whether it is learning to knit, eating well, running, or creating routines— you need to invest in your wellbeing.

Look at how you spend your days. Are you using every opportunity to maximise your ability to be awesome? Every opportunity means every meal, every conversation, every hour sleeping (or not), every run or walk that you do (or don't do). Over the next week, map out what you spend each hour doing. Include not just your work day, but every hour you are awake. At the end of the week, look at how you spent your time and ask yourself these questions:

- How much time did I spend doing paid work?
- How much time did I spend doing unpaid work (things that are still work, like cleaning the house)?
- How much time did I spend doing things I really enjoyed?
- How much time did I spend doing things I did not really need to do?
- How much time did I not use as well as I could (like scrolling through Facebook)?
- How much sleep did I actually get?

Looking hard at how you spend your time means you might want to make some different choices. Then it is time to swing into action:

- Schedule time in your day for exercise. It doesn't have to be training for a marathon—walking is great for the mind and body. Get off the bus a few stops earlier, or make a habit of parking a couple of blocks away from where you need to go.
- Think about what you are eating. There are endless books and materials online to help you eat well.
- Aim to learn something new at least each month. Read a book on a topic you know nothing about, visit somewhere new, join a club, take a night class.
- At least once a month, meet and talk to people with different backgrounds and experiences from you. Listen and learn from what they have to say. Be open to having your views challenged.
- Find ways of making your routines work for you. Taking control over morning routines can take stress out of your day.
- Take sleeping seriously and work hard at doing it.

Make work work

This thing called work—whatever form it may take—takes a lot of our time and energy, and it can eat away at our health and wellbeing. Not having work when we want it also takes up a lot of our time and energy.

So much of our identity can be tied up with what we do—that is, where we work and what we do there. Our answer to the question 'So what do you do?' helps other people place us in our social order. Some jobs come with prestige, others don't.

I was surprised that one of the things I found hardest when I left the role of chief executive to set up a portfolio career was how to answer that question: 'So what do you do?' I always felt like replying, 'Well, take a seat, because this is going to take a while.' I work on a range of projects and have a number of roles, but they are all focused on achieving specific goals— and explaining that concisely can be difficult over a glass of chardonnay. It took talking to colleagues with similar portfolio careers to help me find the short answer, but I still stumble sometimes and grimace when the question is asked.

Work is a large part of our lives not just because of the time we spend doing it, but also because it is so closely linked to our personal identities. So making work work for us is important.

There is a lot of discussion today about achieving work–life balance. Some people consider work as separate from life, which is not always a helpful way of thinking if work is a key part of your life—waiting until after work to live would be quite tragic. Other people say it is critical to think about how much you work and how you prioritise your time, and to make sure your priorities provide balance in your life.

With the technology that is part of our lives today it is often difficult to separate work from the rest of life. Most of us are able to be connected to our work 24/7, and it is all too easy to be trapped by the continual stream of emails, and to give in to expectations of instant replies. We can respond to an email or text at any time, and well beyond the physical boundaries of any office. Technology means we are more controlled by our work; the new workplace is anywhere that we are, be it at home, at the supermarket, or in the playground.

Some companies, and even whole countries, are working on policies to manage this (like deleting emails that arrive when an employee is on holiday). In 2017 the French government passed a law requiring companies with more than 50 employees to establish hours when staff should not send or answer emails. The aim was to ensure employees are fairly paid for their work, and to prevent burnout by protecting private time. French legislator Benoit Hamon described the law as an answer for employees who 'leave the office, but they do not leave their work. They remain attached by a kind of electronic leash—like a dog.'[4]

> **Most of us are able to be connected to our work 24/7, and it is all too easy to be trapped by the continual stream of emails, and to give in to expectations of instant replies.**

Many companies have flexible work policies, but whether they are able to be implemented is another question. Others don't trust that staff working at home will actually work, and some have cultures where being at your desk until after 6pm is crucial to being seen as an effective employee. For people on shift work or who have client-driven deadlines, flexible work is unlikely to be possible.

What work means for you

So, making work *work* is fraught. But your starting point should be having a clear view of what work means for you. Your ideal may be not to work at all but to build that vintage car from the spare parts that are cluttering up your garage, or to work less and spend more time with your kids.

It may not always be possible to achieve exactly what you want, but by thinking hard about the things you can control about your work and actively seeking to change some of these you can put yourself back in the driver's seat.

For Michelle Dickinson, mastering saying 'No' was a critical part of making work work for her. She has found a way to navigate requests for her input that works well: 'I used to really struggle with saying no, and I just found myself overworked, stretching everything, so I wasn't good for anybody. Now I actually say to people, "I would love to help you, but these are my measures of success in what I do"—I only say yes to things that actually directly align with the objectives that I have for my purpose in this world.

> **Your ideal may be not to work at all but to build that vintage car from the spare parts that are cluttering up your garage, or to work less and spend more time with your kids.**

'You're not offending the person, you're not saying, "Your project isn't just as worthy." You're saying, "It doesn't align, and here are my stated goals and this is why it doesn't align."'

Dan Khan thinks hard about the concept of balancing the priorities in his life. As an entrepreneur, he can see that some work projects eat into family life but that he can make a conscious choice to do this because there is a longer-term pay-off. But he also puts in place a check. Each month he stops, takes stock of all areas of his life, and checks where he needs to put his focus. This allows him to maintain a balanced perspective, consistently reminding himself of his priorities.

He argues that his business success has come from having strong support systems around him—his wife and son. He sees others who do not have such systems in place for themselves and he believes that this is something we should talk about more often.

'There are entrepreneurs, relatively high-profile ones that I talk to, their company's doing awesomely well, but have they got family and healthy relationships and marriages behind them? Probably not. I think it's important just to keep that stuff in perspective and come back and check yourself.'

There have been many times over the years when work choices have influenced where in the world David and his family lived. Each time an opportunity has arisen he and his wife have had a reality check and a conversation about whether it makes sense. Even though they may not always have the same priorities, they have approached their life together and their respective high-pressure careers as a team. This means they integrate work and life and see it as one long adventure of discovery.

As an exercise in creative expression, try writing down or drawing (or write a song if you are like David) what your ideal working day, week and year would look like:

- How much time are you spending on paid work?
- What are you doing in your paid work?
- What are you doing in the time that you are not paid for?

Then assess how far away you are from your ideal:

- Do you want more or less paid work?
- Do you want different types of paid work?
- Do you want your working week to be different? Your year to be different?

Ask yourself what steps you can take to make work work better for you now and in the future:

- What financial plans do you need to put in place to make changes?
- What skills or experiences do you need to get you where you want to go?
- What help do you need from others?

I did this exercise a few years ago by drawing a circle on a piece of paper. I divided the circle into segments, like an orange, that represented how much time I spent in family time, paid work, unpaid work (like housework), volunteer work, friends, and leisure. Looking at it, I realised that I wanted to spend less time in unpaid work, less time in paid work, more time with family and more time exercising. As a result I employed a cleaner and, while it took me a few years to get there, moved to a portfolio career that gives me a 'better return' on the amount of time I spend on paid work. As a consultant, I now spend less time in meetings and more time working on the issues I care about.

Ages and stages

Looking back on the last two decades of my work, I have to chuckle about how out of step my career was with my stage in life. Straight out of university and into the workplace I wanted to take up every challenge going. I was looking to my work for stretch and excitement. Having just completed a Master's degree while working delivering pizzas meant I had had no free time for several years and I was used to working hard all day and night. In contrast, the workplace seemed a bit slow and as a junior analyst the work was on the dull side.

Fast-forward ten years, and with two young children, leadership opportunities were increasingly available to me, with the excitement, challenge and responsibility that came with them. But they came just at the time when disrupted sleep and chicken pox ruled, and having a nice cup of tea and an early night were far more appealing than excitement.

Now, having made a deliberate choice to make it so, my career and life stage are more in sync. But it took twenty years to get there. Navigating between work and our stage in life is a tricky thing, but the lessons shared by the people we interviewed show that a degree of planning and anticipating can help us flourish at each stage of our life and career, now and in the future.

Dan Khan, with a background in start-ups, says that before he had a family he would work long hours. Often he would have a job, and then after hours he would be working on his next business. Now, with a family, he has learnt that juggling works, and the world does not end if you step back from a work project.

Linda Clark has a powerful way of thinking about her career and life stage. Her career pathway has changed, but her ambition has not. As a mother, ensuring she meets her children's needs means she has to be agile, and it will affect how and what she is working on. But that does not mean she is not ambitious or planning for her future of work. She is anticipating the time when her work may become more central and is thinking about how to prepare for this.

'I feel like that window, that space is opening and I can own those thoughts again. I'm in that nice place actually, where I'm just getting that sensation of the possibility, because two more years and they will be finished school. At the moment, I'm just enjoying the prospect—it's just like a little bit of sunlight coming through the doorway—and I'm thinking, what's that going to be?'

Shay Wright recognises that he is at a stage of his life when he has fewer responsibilities towards others than he may have in the future, which drives him to use his time wisely now. He knows that he is free to pursue his ambitions, and that he had better get going because this may change.

'At the moment I have no one relying upon me except myself. Many people do not have that situation: people have kids, people have parents they have to look after, they have siblings who need help, they have other whānau or responsibilities, but I don't have that. I have those people, but they are living healthy and happy lives themselves, so I'm not relied upon. I think that frees me up emotionally, mentally, to just focus on pursuing the things that I feel are important.'

Both Linda Clark and Rachel Taulelei observe specific pressures and expectations on mothers in the workplace. Rachel comments that women often ask her about how she juggles her various roles and commitments. The juggling of many balls can fall disproportionately to women. Not many men are asked this question, she suggests.

Linda knows how fraught it can be in the phase of navigating your career when your children are younger, with people assuming you are no longer ambitious or have lost the drive to be successful—neither of which is likely to be true. She says this often comes up when she is asked about her future career intentions. She will give an answer, but also knows it will depend on her children's needs.

'Every child's different, every child's needs are different—that means that when you're a mother and you're asked, "What are you going to do in five years?" you hedge your bets because it depends. How old are my kids? What stage are they going to be in? Even if they're at an age where you think it's safe for me to be more hands-off, what if it's a bad year at school? What if I have a daughter who develops anorexia? What if I have a kid who has a mountain-bike accident?'

Now that their son has grown up and left home, David and his wife Yvonne are what marketers call 'empty nesters', with more time for other pursuits. They have learned how to integrate work and life and negotiate priorities, but this has taken years to perfect.

> Navigating your career when your children
> are younger can be fraught, with people
> assuming you are no longer ambitious
> or have lost the drive to be successful—
> neither of which is likely to be true.

Different phases of our lives will bring different needs and wants from our work. There is no easy checklist or silver bullet for working this out—you will notice that there is no bullet-point list of actions at the end of this section. Making work work across our different life stages is about acknowledging and planning for this. Those we interviewed emphasised the need to be agile, to be able to change gear depending on circumstances. This puts us in the best position to enjoy each stage of our life and career. This is wise advice as it challenges our mindset. Our *why* and our ambition may not change, but how we express these at different times in our careers may do.

Stay positive and build resilience

One of the funniest moments during Linda Clark's interview was when she talked about a court session she had been in the day before. She knew the evidence she was presenting wasn't as strong as it could be, but that was what she had to work with. The High Court judge she was in front of let her know his views of her work. With a smile, Linda took it on the chin and moved on, but she noted that had this happened ten years earlier, she would have ended up in tears in the women's toilets.

Resilience—the ability to accept setbacks, pick yourself up quickly and get moving again—is a skill we all need now, and one we will definitely need more of in the future.

> **Being unsuccessful is not a measure of how capable a person is, or their personal worth. It just means that someone else is more aligned to the criteria or has more experience.**

During a meeting with a group of young women leaders I was asked how best to cope with applying for a job and not being successful. My answer was that I have had a lot of practice in being turned down—that is actually a measure of success. Over my career I have had the courage to apply and then apply again.

I reminded the young women in the group about the processes of recruitment from an employer's perspective. There are usually many CVs in the pile, and they are judged and matched against a set of criteria. Being unsuccessful is not a measure of how capable a person is, or their personal worth. It just means that someone else is more aligned to the criteria or has more experience.

But my key message to the young woman was that what really matters is how you manage yourself when you are not successful. How fast and strongly you bounce back and start your next job application is the true measure of success. It is about staying positive and being resilient.

Resilience can be developed

The good news is that resilience can be developed and built. Staying positive and optimistic, developing the ability to manage strong and difficult emotions, and having a good support network around you—these are all ways to become more resilient.[5] Of course, this is easy to say but not so easy to do. Work cultures are filled with stress, speed and increasing complexity, all of which challenge and wear down our resilience every day. A study of British workers found that 75 per cent of them thought the biggest drain on their resilience reserves was managing difficult work colleagues or office politics.[6]

While the forces that are likely to wear down your resilience are hard to avoid, there are practical strategies that can be adopted to help you stay positive and build resilience.

- Rachel Petero thinks about her emotional resilience like a muscle, and just like a physical muscle she needs to keep building it. She finds that putting herself in a diverse range of environments and circumstances where she feels uncomfortable works to build her resilience muscle, keeping her on her toes so she can be prepared for the unexpected.
- Linda Clark uses the technique of compartmental- ising. When things go wrong, she can mentally park the issue in a cupboard in her mind. This allows her not to carry fear, disputes or mistakes close to her and not to take any baggage forward. She also does this with interactions with people who are not supportive

or could erode her confidence. While she may have to continue to work with them, she tucks the interaction away. Her supportive friends and networks help her in the compartmentalising process by reminding her of the importance of locking a recent mistake in its rightful closet in her mind.

- One of Joshua Vial's approaches to staying positive is similar. He describes his technique as managing the 'self-talk'—the things he is telling himself. Rather than dwelling on negative thoughts, he chooses to move on and think about something else.

- Selina Tusitala Marsh uses the 'Morning Pages' technique to control her negative thoughts and capture her creativity. She starts each morning writing free-form in her journal, capturing all her negative and disruptive thoughts. Writing these thoughts down makes them diminish, leaving her with a free mind with which to focus on her creative work.

Sometimes we need others to remind us of our skills and talents when we are focused on our weaknesses and failures. There are times when we can see only the problems in front of us, but while things may be hard for us this is often the beginning of something positive. How often have people told you that being made redundant was the best thing that happened to their career? Friends and family can help us reframe our circumstances, and surrounding ourselves with people who back us and support us is important.

While we need cheerleaders who will point out our strengths, we also need space to ourselves. Nearly all the people interviewed talked about the importance of creating space for themselves in which to think, take a breather and regroup. Selina Tusitala Marsh builds time in her weekend when she can take her kayak out on the sea. She knows she needs some time alone and that this refuels her. For Joshua Vial, it is about realising when he needs a change of scene and then taking action.

> **Sometimes we need others to remind us of our skills and talents when we are focused on our weaknesses and failures.**

Understanding where we draw our strength from is also important. In the study of British workers mentioned above, the researchers asked where they thought resilience came from. Around 90 per cent said their resilience came from themselves, and half thought also from their social relationships and networks.[7] Finding time to refuel and stay connected to your friends and family is important.

Giving back to others and actively contributing to a community or activity that is bigger than yourself is also important for staying positive and building resilience. For a number of years David has made a point of working on a voluntary basis with not-for-profit organisations, giving him an opportunity to share his governance experience. In helping others he usually learns a lot.

Selina talks about how giving feeds the soul: 'Giving back to the community in some way, shape or form, no matter what your job is, just feeds the civic spirit and feeds the community, feeds our nation, feeds our world. No matter what you do, if you can find a way to help in some way, shape or form, then you are going to get back so much more.'

We often think that being resilient means marching on through adversity, picturing images of mud-caked soldiers and rugby players battling against the odds. Perhaps we believe that the longer we manage to tough it out, the more successful we are. But researchers have found that if we do not have some sort of recovery time we will not be successful.

Giving back to others and actively contributing to a community or activity that is bigger than yourself is also important for staying positive and building resilience.

One key to being resilient is to work hard and then stop, take a break, and then start again. Taking a break enables us to stay more motivated and be more productive. But taking a break means really taking a break. In order for our brains to recover we need to stop them being aroused, so that we can rest and get our energy back. Just stopping reading your emails does not mean you are really taking a break—you are probably still thinking about work. In order to be resilient we need proper mental breaks.[8]

Dr Sven Hansen is the founder of The Resilience Institute, which offers both training courses and coaching in resilience. He defines resilience as the learned ability to demonstrate four characteristics:

1. Bounce—responding constructively to adversity, finding ways to emerge stronger and more effective.
2. Courage—embracing the future with a curious mind, an open heart, and the will to take action.
3. Connection—a respectful engagement with our

bodies, our emotions, our thoughts and our purpose, extending to family, friends, community, workplace and beyond.

4. Creativity—aligning our talents and skills with a meaningful challenge.[9]

Building resilience in our young people and in ourselves

There is increasing awareness of the need to build resilience in our young people as they come under pressure from the ever-growing number of choices and changes in the world around them. Common mental health issues, including anxiety and depression, often appear first during adolescence and can have a serious effect on students' behaviour, learning and achievement. Unfortunately New Zealand has not solved this challenge, and has one of the highest teen suicide rates in the developed world. Initiatives such as the My FRIENDS Youth Resilience Programme, Sparklers and Res-Kids are welcome developments as we try to address this important issue.[10]

Academic studies show that self-esteem and resilience are significant predictors of academic performance, as well as social and emotional wellbeing.[11] Careers New Zealand emphasises resilience in its Student Career Management Competencies,[12] and organisations such as Like Minds, Like Mine[13] have been set up to provide much-needed support.

Organisations as well as individuals need resilience, and today it is written into many corporate documents. There are a lot of training opportunities where you can learn to build resilience, but there are also a lot of things you can do on your own to help you focus on staying positive and building your own resilience:

- Put yourself in circumstances where you are out of your comfort zone. This will keep you on your toes, and you will keep building ways to manage yourself through change.
- Find ways of dealing with setbacks. It is normal to be disappointed or angry in these situations, but staying that way is not useful. Find ways of moving on.
- Manage your negative thoughts. What you say to yourself impacts on your actions and your ability to succeed. Managing what happens in your head matters. Use a technique like journaling to help.
- Surround yourself with positive, supportive people who will encourage you, help you to put setbacks into perspective, and challenge any negative ideas you have about yourself.
- Take time out. Having some time to yourself to think, plan and regroup can help keep you positive.

The last word here goes to Frances Valintine. She knows that by working on things she believes in her confidence, resilience and positivity will not only be maintained, but will grow.

'If you told me to go and talk about or do something I'm not passionate about, I would absolutely walk away. I'm confident with things that I believe in, know and understand really well.'

With this thought, Frances takes us full circle back to the beginning of this book. If you are clear about what you care about—if you know your *why*—you will be working from a position of strength. You will attract people who will help and support you; you will plan and be open to opportunities; and you will find ways to stay positive and be resilient.

THE RETRAINED JUGGERNAUT
LINDA CLARK

After many years as one of New Zealand's leading political journalists, Linda Clark retrained as a lawyer. She now works in a public law team, managing complex legal, political and regulatory relationships.

For Linda, finding a pathway for her career and her commitments as a mother has been an important theme in the more recent phases of her career. Her career changes have been informed by her analysis of the industries and environments within which she works, and the needs of her children.

'Once my children were born, I went to radio for four years, and that was a launch pad because it was more stable, you didn't have to travel. I loved it, could have done it for a lot longer. I'd just hit forty and I thought, what am I going to do for the next twenty-five to thirty years? This is not an industry that is about longevity. Which isn't to say—I mean there are people who last a long time in radio—but if you're kind of a restless spirit, there are not many other places to go.'

Retraining as a lawyer in her forties brought a range of reactions.

'That was a real lurch in a different direction, and that's been fantastic in lots of ways. Very tricky, though, to make the transition. A lot of my peers and those older than me didn't really think I was serious: it was like a hormonal crisis—some middle-aged woman goes and does a degree, to pep up her brain or something. But then others were just fantastic and really got it, were really supportive and mentoring and have made it all possible.'

> 'You go from being the top of your game
> and then you start in a new thing and all
> that muscle memory doesn't exist.'

Changing careers was harder than she expected.

'It was hard because a law degree is a really hard thing to get, and working in the law is really challenging. Journalism is a craft and it took me a long time to get really good at that. The law is a craft, and it takes a long time to get on top of your skills, and you've got to be a bit patient about that. You go from being the top of your game and then you start in a new thing and all that muscle memory doesn't exist.'

Linda has had to face negative stereotypes about middle-aged women.

'Unconscious bias against middle-aged women is everywhere. Wherever we go, the assumption is we'll hardly be able to function on our phones; we won't be able to use our computers; we won't know anything that's current. We will make safe choices. We'll be happy to be quiet. If everyone in the room thinks you're mumsy, then it is really gut-wrenchingly negative. The ions in the air are negative. That stuff you've got to deal with.'

Moving from what Linda describes as 'one dying industry to another' has made her think a lot about what she will be doing in the future.

'I've gone into an archaic profession. The law firms will have to change. The way they charge will have to change. The way they're structured will have to change. It's going to be really hard for the young ones to get the experience. A lot of challenges are in store for the profession. But in the end, people will still need wise counsel, and that's what I give. I've got a good brain, a lot of life experience—I can help you through it. I'm confident that the skill is still required.'

THE CREATIVE FORCE
SELINA TUSITALA MARSH

 Associate Professor Selina Tusitala Marsh is an Auckland-based Pasifika poet and scholar who is of Samoan, Tuvaluan, English, Scottish and French descent. She was the first person of Pacific descent to graduate with a PhD in English from the University of Auckland, where she now lectures in both creative writing and Māori and Pacific literary studies. Her work has been widely published and has appeared in a range of books, online and hard-copy literary journals, and websites. Selina is New Zealand's Poet Laureate for 2017–2019.

Selina's career journey may have taken place mostly in one institution—a university—but it has been a journey with many milestones. The first one was about being comfortable with working in a university setting and finding a way to be herself in an environment where she did not feel as if she fitted in.

'It took me years to feel that I could truly be my

authentic self in this institution, because there was a certain way of being, thinking, looking and sounding that didn't reflect me. Even more hostile were ideologies that marginalised difference, that placed little value on what I did and, more importantly, how I did it. You can start feeling embattled and resentful. I just want to thrive. I want to be spirit-centred, culturally intact, and thrive in this place. Maya Angelou defines success as "liking yourself, liking what you do, and liking how you do it". It has taken me years to get there.'

Another milestone in her journey was finding her own pathway forward, when she was raised to do as she was directed.

'You're the first this, you're the first that, and so you come in wearing quite a heavy mantle of representation. And walking away isn't an option—although some in my position did choose to walk away from the institution. It was too alienating for them, and certainly there were easier ways to make a living. But I wasn't brought up to see that as an option. During my postgrad years Albert Wendt was my mentor, along with Witi Ihimaera. They were both saying, "You need to occupy this space when we go, because there's nobody behind you and you need to continue the work." I didn't question it. I didn't really know what I wanted to do at 23, but I didn't question their certainty in my ability and my responsibility to the Māori and Pacific community. I now see that I did have a choice.'

Selina has learned to manage and embrace her contradictions and accept herself.

'The thing that makes you different, that makes you stand out in the crowd, the thing that you're so self-conscious about when younger, when you're trying desperately to conform—that will be the thing that holds the potential to represent your unique power, your difference. For me it has always been my hair. I got teased about my wild, unruly mane a lot. I got called "mophead", "gollywog". Over the years my big, frizzy hair has morphed into part of my identity—one that symbolises my mana. I've learned that by accepting, embracing and enhancing your difference, you accept, embrace and enhance your life. If I could get that sixteen-year-old girl to instead think, "I'm going to wear it out, I'm not going to plait it, I'm not going to squeeze it into a tight bun—I'm going to let it fly," that would be a victory. But that's all part of the journey, knowing yourself and accepting yourself.'

She celebrates that she has achieved confidence in her unique creative voice and cultural capital.

'Sometimes, you have to fake it until you make it. I was in a taxi on my way to a literary festival with a pre-eminent Pākehā literary scholar and writer, and some other literary notables. He asked the taxi driver a really dumb question. I had this epiphany that the only difference between us was confidence—and the fact that this society centres his cultural capital. A question is a question—it's not evidence of the inability of his entire people to navigate the elite territory of literary engagement. But that's the mantle of representation I wear. Everything you do is subject, fairly or not, to scrutiny—it's happened to me enough times to make it so every single time I open my mouth publicly. Yes, it comes down to essential issues of worth, but it's not just personal; as a person of Pasifika descent, it's political.'

THE LEGACY BUILDER
RACHEL PETERO

 Rachel Petero brings her entrepreneurial talent and coaching expertise alongside her strong identity with Tainui-Waikato to the table of global organisations. In June 2015, she returned to Aotearoa from Qatar after fifteen years abroad in the UK and Middle East. Rachel successfully led award-winning talent and leadership and gender diversity transformation programmes for graduates, women, and up to board level in multiple industry sectors.

Rachel has created a coaching business with the aim of unleashing the potential of indigenous women. Her driver has been her values, her skills and what she wants to achieve.

'I've got a professional background of HR, working in business and starting my own business—so entrepreneurship. If you pull all that together with my core values that is basically doing what I love on a daily basis. Everything is aligned to my values, to my expertise and the audience that I want to serve.'

She has started her business grounded in her own whānau.

'Taking what I learnt from corporates and asking, how does that fit into community? Then getting others to come on that journey: always taking others with me, because it's too hard and boring doing it alone, and I don't think you can achieve scale when you are alone. And really challenging myself with my whānau and stretching them and saying, "What do you want?" "What do you want?"—to my parents, to my sisters, to my nieces and nephews, to my aunties. What do you want in your life? How can I support you? How can you support yourself? What needs to change for the future to be different? Because if you always do what you've always done . . .'

Rachel has used the principles of Māori culture, and love of her culture, to guide her thinking and future.

'My internal compass, intuition, female GPS is a great way to check in. Traditionally Māori have always planned seven generations ahead. So if I said, "I'm going to go and sell the properties that I have and the land that I have, because I need more money for something for me only"— that wouldn't be aligned to that.'

> **Rachel has used the principles of Māori culture, and love of her culture, to guide her thinking and future.**

The same principles have guided her aspirations for her future work.

'The legacy of what I leave behind is driven by role models like Te Puea, one of our Waikato-Tainui legacy leaders. Her legacy is that she continues to look after the homeless. So by researching role models and other examples of women globally, it is amazing to see how their work continues even today. So how do you do that? You have to do it with others. Bring others with you. Develop and grow your expertise through others. It has to be passed on to live on through others. That's the way to create legacy leaders.

'Yes, there's a financial benefit, and what would I want that financial benefit to do? It would create education, employment, business opportunities, foundations that continue that kind of legacy leadership work that carries on way after my time for indigenous women and their families.'

Rachel is confident that her efforts will pay back over the long term.

'I just think being smart in the way that I invest financially, invest in others, invest in myself—we invest financially, invest in expertise, invest in technology, invest in local and global partnerships, and keep evolving, learning and tweaking the model. All of the work I'm doing around developing indigenous leaders, as long as I stay true to my values, do what my tupuna have done— build, grow and sustain for the future and think beyond today—it will all start to unfold. It's about bringing others on that journey. It's about doing it as a collective.'

CHAPTER 7:
BRING ON
THE FUTURE

Earlier we discussed humans' fascination with the new, and the fact that we have always adapted to and, at a greater or lesser speed, embraced new technology. We looked at what has been called the Fourth Industrial Revolution, and how Moore's Law demonstrates that computer power has developed at an exponential rate. New ideas regarding artificial intelligence and automation are fast becoming reality. The next generation will grow up taking for granted chatbots, autonomous cars and virtual reality—these are all based on technology invented before they were born.

We have looked at how these changes in technology are transforming the way we work. There will be fewer manual jobs in the future, and the old industrial labour contract ('I'll give you steady wages, you give me your five-day week') will have been replaced by the gig economy as employment markets ebb and flow around a multitude of different work options, new roles and evolving industry sectors.

Today's schoolchildren may live to be a hundred and have over 40 'jobs' in their lifetime. Successful people will be lifelong learners, knowing that their competencies and experience need to be constantly updated. Educational institutions will have adapted to a 'learning on demand' model where people take on new knowledge when they need it, not years beforehand. Successful employers will attract and retain great workers by offering them continual challenges and personal development. Effective governments will have developed policies to support both workers and employers as they navigate through continuing changes. Tax settings and social support structures will have evolved.

Robots, artificial intelligence and machine learning are just the latest developments in the history of a species that is extraordinarily curious, inventive and resilient. While technology may be value neutral, humans have the capability to envisage a progressive future and work towards achieving it. The core qualities that have always helped us survive will help us thrive into the future.

Where to from here?

Throughout this book we have demonstrated ways to respond and move forward positively as you prepare for the future of work. Based on expert advice and the experience of positive, thriving New Zealanders, you now have a complete range of tools that will enable you not just to face the future, but to embrace it.

We have looked at ways to:

- explore and identify your *why*, and what your true values are.
- understand the intricacies of your personality and the way your previous life story influences how you think and act.
- plan for the next decades of your work life, leaving plenty of scope for flexibility.
- look after yourself so that you are mentally and physically fit to take on whatever challenges inspire you.

KNOW YOURSELF
Understand your *why*
Know what you value
Live your personal brand
Fail well
Build your confidence
Know what you want

LOOK AFTER YOURSELF
Invest in yourself
Make work work
Stay positive
Build resilience

KNOW WHAT'S AROUND YOU
Escape the echo chamber
Be curious
Understand what's coming
Build your networks
Seek advice

HAVE A PLAN—AND TAKE CHANCES
Confront the future
Set goals
Be open to change
Work hard
Be bold

The challenge now is to take all that information and decide what you are going to do with it. What are your hopes and dreams? How are you going to set about achieving them? It is time for you to take ownership—and take action.

Our advice is to look at these principles and actions as a complete system and put them together so that they form a comprehensive whole. Most people already have some of the answers and are taking some positive action, but don't have a cohesive approach. They may know their values, but they do nothing different as a result. They may have a plan, but it is completely unrealistic when they look at what is around them. They may pursue their goals, but at the expense of their personal health.

What are your hopes and dreams? How are you going to set about achieving them? It is time for you to take ownership—and take action.

There is no 'right' way to act. Each of the people we have featured in the book has their own personal philosophy, set of values, and way of achieving their goals. What they all share is a vision, a belief in themselves, an acceptance that they will face challenges, and the knowledge that nothing comes without hard work.

We asked them: 'What advice would you give your sixteen-year-old self?' We wanted to know what they have learned from their experience of work so far, and what they could mine from that that was worthy of passing on to the next generations. We think that their advice is applicable to everyone who is readying themselves for the future of work, whatever age and stage they are at. This is what they told us.

It's all about people

The key message here is the importance of building relationships, because the human element is something that will never be easily replicated by technology. People will be key to all aspects of your life, including work. For Dan Khan, it was about finding and connecting with people who inspired him. Spending time with these people meant he was encouraged to push himself and achieve more.

Don't settle early (or ever) on a specific job

Looking back, Shay Wright sees that testing a variety of different jobs and working in a range of organisations gave him a great start. He believes that a portfolio career is a good way to start out in work. Generating multiple revenue streams reduces the risk of losing your job, while working across a range of jobs allows you to test and try things, and you can build your skills while earning.

Joshua Vial has similar advice. Try lots of roles and seek experiences. Find things that you love and then find ways of making money from them. This strategy is currently working well for Jo. She has identified three areas where she wants to work to enact social change, and she has built a portfolio career around these areas.

Dan Khan says that working in a range of roles provides the basics you may need if you ever want to start your own business, as well as making you more effective in your preferred role. He believes that to build his skills as an excellent computer programmer, the best thing he did was work as a marketer and in sales for a computer firm. In these roles he got to understand what the customer wanted and how to sell a product. It made his development work more customer-focused. It also meant that when he did start his own business he understood the value of marketing, and he knew how to establish this function effectively.

Keep investing in your learning

All those we interviewed advocated for the power and importance of lifelong learning. Just because you have finished your formal learning, that doesn't mean your education is complete. Ongoing learning, whether through self-directed web courses, on-the-job training, or whatever form works for you, needs to be part of your future. Informal learning relationships, for example, can be established with mentors. This is something that Shay has found to be very powerful.

> Ongoing learning, whether through self-directed web courses, on-the-job training, or whatever form works for you, needs to be part of your future.

Dan Khan argues that we don't know what we don't know, and that we have to always be open to learning, including asking for help and guidance. Over a career with twenty or more different jobs, young people will need to become experts in different roles over and over again. Continually refining how to learn will be a key to future success. Frances Valintine agrees, and points out that it has never been easier to access education. There are many free online courses, for example— all it takes to complete them is determination and discipline.

In her role as a university lecturer, Selina Tusitala Marsh has observed that many students focus on getting grades and doing what they need to pass their assessments. Many secondary school teachers will recognise this behaviour. She laments that this is such a dominant form of learning, which should not always be about working out what is needed to pass an exam. Learning needs to include exploring and being curious, not just focusing on the end grade. Investing in your learning may include achieving formal qualifications, but it should also involve exploring new areas of knowledge.

Find your *why* and follow your passion

Taking the time to reflect and work out what really interests you may sound simple, even obvious, but how many of us actually do it? How many of us instead do what is expected of us or what we assume is the right thing?

While many people may give you advice, you are the best judge of what is the right pathway for you. Vivien Maidaborn describes the sweet spot we should all aspire to and encourage our young people to search out—where you love what you are doing and the market will pay you for doing it.

Michelle Dickinson advises that the easiest way to find this spot is to start with your strengths and passions, as well as an honest assessment of your weaknesses and dislikes, and home in on what you really care about. In her view, you must assume that robots will take over many tasks that are currently done by humans, but your strength will come from finding your value and the contribution you can make.

Don't expect linear

In the future it will be rare for someone to train as a lawyer and then work as a lawyer. Most of those we interviewed said that when they looked back at their career there was little linear progression. This trend will continue and intensify. You will need to be flexible, adaptable, and able to find your path as your environment changes.

Try hard and back yourself

When Rachel Taulelei looks back over her career, she singles out one thing that has made her successful. She tried hard— at everything. Whatever she was doing, she was determined to give it her all. With this philosophy, you can always hold your head high, and have the integrity that comes with giving something your all.

Along with this comes backing and believing in yourself. Trust your intuition—in times when a decision is difficult or you are challenged, you will not be alone, your instinct will be right there.

Trust that the thing that makes you stand out in the crowd will come to represent you for all the right reasons. For Selina Tusitala Marsh, this was her hair. Growing up, she tried to hide her masses of black curls. Now she wears her hair down and long as a proud symbol of who she is and where she comes from.

Give back

Josh points out that being successful at work is often judged by what we earn and how much we can consume as a result of that. He has found that he has gained the most satisfaction in his work when he has been able to help others. This is true for many of the people we interviewed.

Change has a long history

We have canvassed a lot of ideas and people in our exploration of the future world of work. We have looked at some grim predictions, including statistics that show millions of jobs are disappearing around the world. But we remain optimistic and excited about the future, and your part in it.

The most important piece of work you can do is to work on yourself. Be prepared to disrupt your thought patterns and your daily routines in the search for new, better approaches and opportunities.

Without doubt the changes happening in the workplace and to the workforce are massive, rapid and far-reaching. The consequences of automation and artificial intelligence, along with new developments yet to arrive, will lead to new ways of working that no one can forecast with any certainty. As someone once said, though there is disagreement about who said it first, 'The future isn't what it used to be.'[1]

The most important piece of work you can do is to work on yourself. Be prepared to disrupt your thought patterns and your daily routines in the search for new, better approaches and opportunities. Seek out new skills and experiences. Learn to embrace change rather than avoid or ignore it. Enjoy the different people you meet and the problems you solve along the way.

Societies and humans have faced, and successfully navigated, periods of massive change before. An early YouTube clip, best known as 'Norwegian monks', provides a humorous reminder that we have gone through similar cycles of fear, response, trial and confidence many times throughout history when new technology has disrupted our lives. Set in the Middle Ages, the clip shows a monk consulting the local helpdesk to help him make the difficult transition from scrolls to books. He is both scared and amazed by the new technology. We recommend you check it out.[2]

The four principles we have explored in this book—the four principles identified by the people we interviewed as key things that will prepare you to be successful in the future—are timeless. They are about the core human skills and attitudes that have carried us through change in the past and will do so again in the future.

Know yourself

Scholars have long preached the value of self-knowledge.

> *He who knows others is wise;*
> *he who knows himself is enlightened.*
> —LAO TZU (C. SIXTH CENTURY BC)

> *No one is free who has not obtained the empire of himself.*
> *No man is free who cannot command himself.*
> —PYTHAGORAS (C. 570–495 BC)

> *This above all: to thine own self be true, And it must follow, as*
> *the night the day, Thou canst not then be false to any man.*
> —WILLIAM SHAKESPEARE (1564–1616)

There is a well-known Māori proverb, 'Ka muri, ka mua', meaning 'Look back to look forward'. This has also been expressed as 'walking backwards into the future', signifying the practice in

Māoridom of referencing past culture and history when taking a look into the future. Understanding where you have come from is essential to understanding where you want to go.

In a world of rapid change, it has never been more important to hold on to who you are, understand your *why*, and live according to clearly expressed values. These are the bedrock truths that will help you keep strong during times when your confidence is damaged or a project fails.

> **In a world of rapid change, it has never been more important to hold on to who you are, understand your *why*, and live according to clearly expressed values.**

They are also the signposts you need to share with others—colleagues, friends, family—to help them understand you and support you to achieve your full potential.

Know what's around you

One of the greatest capabilities that we have now built into computers is one of humanity's oldest skill sets—pattern recognition. Thousands of years living on the African plains helped our ancestors evolve brains that applied sophisticated 'programs' to identify potential food sources and respond to threats from predators. This is a set of skills that we all carry around, mostly unconsciously.

These skills can be focused on the parts of our lives that are productive or the hours that we just while away. We can spend our time guessing the plot of the latest soap series, or following celebrity lifestyles, or we can apply our thinking to the patterns of our work, our relationships and our future.

Be curious, seek out people and ideas that challenge your beliefs, learn all you can about the things that interest you. It has never been easier to access knowledge, and there are plenty of people who will be willing to share their experience with you—to mentor, coach and sponsor you, or simply give you five minutes of their time to chew over an idea.

Have a plan, but take chances

History has always involved individuals and groups making plans and calculating risk versus reward. Māori are proudly descended from adventurers who left their island homelands during the great Polynesian migration, with no guarantee of safe harbour. Later settlers in New Zealand, whether they arrived by boat in the nineteenth century or passed through airport immigration just yesterday, have also made judgements on the positive opportunities and the risks of taking a chance on a new life.

There is risk in doing something, and in doing nothing. Mark Zuckerberg, the co-founder of Facebook, acknowledges great advice from fellow billionaire Peter Thiel: 'The biggest risk is not taking any risk. In a world that is changing really quickly, the only strategy that is guaranteed to fail is not taking risks.'[3]

The best way to mitigate risks and safeguard against failure is to have a plan. Set some goals that take you forward a week, a month, a year or longer, then work hard to achieve them. Be open to change that may be beyond your control, and flexible enough to adapt your plan on the fly. Embrace opportunities— if in doubt, be bold.

Look after yourself

This should be a given—we all share a survival instinct. Yet it is all too easy to neglect our physical, emotional and mental needs, especially during times of stress and change. We all face challenges and get knocked down, but if we take care of ourselves, nourish our bodies and our minds and work on developing resilience it is much easier to get up again. It is when you are under stress that you most need to take some time to reflect on how you are feeling and what you can do to remove negative influences from your life. In the pursuit of happiness, health beats wealth every time.

Bring on the future

When it comes to stimulating interest, novelty is a strong attractor. New beats old. But when it comes to preparing ourselves for the future we should always take the past with us as a guide and a supporter. Humans have survived massive changes to their lives and their work for centuries. We will do so again.

Michelle Dickinson: 'We're living in a really disruptive time where the jobs that we *always* thought would exist forever actually are not going to exist very soon, and it's going to be really scary. Make sure you take a look around at what you do and figure out if it's aligning with your strengths and your passions, and never forget the human side of what you do—because we're moving into an age where technology is *literally* going to be taking jumps, but it's never going to take the human connection side of that jump. Remember that we're still going to need humans to interact with humans.'

ACKNOWLEDGEMENTS

We would like to express our appreciation to the following people, without whom this project would not have been possible.

Thanks to our wonderful publisher Allen & Unwin, especially Melanie Laville-Moore for letting us pitch our idea and Jenny Hellen for guiding us through the writing and publishing process. Thanks also to Susan Brierley and Leanne McGregor for their skilful editorial assistance, Abba Renshaw and Becky Innes for their expertise in publicity and marketing, and Kate Barraclough for her excellent design.

Thanks to Melissa Harsant at Capital Transcriptions for typing up our interviews; Yvonne Glover, Byron Glover and Mike Waterman for reading and commenting on early drafts; Murray Bain and Richard Norman for providing helpful references about the future of work; and Dame Wendy Pye for contributing the Foreword.

Last but not least, our warm thanks to the twelve inspiring—and thriving—people who shared their lives and opinions with us, resulting in a rich brew of experience and advice: Brian Steele, Dan Khan, Frances Valintine, Holona Lui, Joshua Vial,

Linda Clark, Dr Michelle Dickinson, Rachel Petero, Rachel Taulelei, Associate Professor Selina Tusitala Marsh, Shay Wright and Vivien Maidaborn.

NOTES

Chapter 1: Work, but not as we know it

1   World Intellectual Property Organization (WIPO), 'Record Year for International Patent Applications in 2016', <www.wipo.int/pressroom/en/articles/2017/article_0002.html>, 15 March 2017.

2   World Economic Forum, 'The Future of Jobs: Employment, skills and workforce strategy for the Fourth Industrial Revolution', Geneva: WEF, 2016.

3   WEF, 'The Future of Jobs'.

4   Carl Benedikt Frey & Michael A. Osborne, 'The Future of Employment: How susceptible are jobs to computerisation?', Working Paper, Oxford: Oxford Martin Programme on Technology and Employment, 2013.

5   Chartered Accountants Australia and New Zealand and the New Zealand Institute of Economic Research, 'Disruptive Technologies: Risks, Opportunities—Can New Zealand make the most of them?', Chartered Accountants Australia and New Zealand, 2015.

6   World Bank, 'World Development Report 2016: Digital Dividends', <www.worldbank.org/en/publication/wdr2016>, 17 May 2016.

7   For more on Singularity University see https://su.org/about/.

8   Tao Lin, 'Human Augmentation Will Change Our Futures: MYOB', <www.stuff.co.nz/business/industries/79711532/human-augmentation-will-change-our-futures-myob>, 9 May 2016.

9   Harold Jarche, 'The Future of Human Work', <https://jarche.com/2016/03/the-future-of-human-work/>, 14 March 2016.

10 Mark Osborne, presentation to Unitec Institute of Technology, 14 July 2017.

11 Lynda Gratton & Andrew Scott, *The 100-Year Life: Living and working in an age of longevity*, London: Bloomsbury, 2016.

12 Foundation for Young Australians, *The New Work Smarts: Thriving in the new work order*, Sydney: FYA, 2017.

13 Foundation for Young Australians, *The New Work Mindset*, Sydney: FYA, 2017.

14 Foundation for Young Australians, *The New Basics: Big data reveals the skills young people need for the New Work Order*, Sydney: FYA, 2017.

15 Krista Pahkin, 'Staying Well in an Unstable World of Work: Prospective cohort study of the determinants of employee well-being', Finnish Institute of Occupational Health, <https://helda.helsinki.fi/bitstream/handle/10138/153421/stayingw.pdf?sequence=1>, 2015.

Chapter 2: How technology is impacting on work

1 CB Insights, 'AI Will Put 10 Million Jobs At High Risk', <www.cbinsights.com/research/jobs-automation-artificial-intelligence-risk>, 6 October 2017.

2 James Manyika, Michael Chui, Mehdi Miremadi et al., 'Harnessing Automation for a Future That Works', McKinsey Global Institute, <www.mckinsey.com/global-themes/digital-disruption/harnessing-automation-for-a-future-that-works>, January 2017.

3 Cate Cadell & Adam Jourdan, 'China Aims to Become World Leader in AI, Challenges U.S. Dominance', <www.reuters.com/article/us-china-ai/china-aims-to-become-world-leader-in-ai-challenges-u-s-dominance-idUSKBN1A5103>, 20 July 2017.

4 Deloitte, '2017 Deloitte Global Human Capital Trends: Rewriting the rules for the digital age', Deloitte University Press, <www2.deloitte.com/content/dam/Deloitte/us/Documents/human-capital/hc-2017-global-human-capital-trends-us.pdf>, 2017.

5 Michael Hayward & Chris Hutching, 'Self-driving Electric Shuttles To Be Made in Christchurch', <www.stuff.co.nz/business/96742431/selfdriving-electric-shuttles-to-be-made-in-christchurch>, 12 September 2017.

6 Salim Ismail, with Michael S. Malone & Yuri van Geest, *Exponential Organizations: Why new organizations are ten times better, faster, and cheaper than yours (and what to do about it)*, New York: Diversion Books, 2014, p. 33.

7 Clayton M. Christensen, *The Innovator's Dilemma: When new technologies cause great firms to fail*, Boston, MA: Harvard Business School Press, 1997.

8   CB Insights, 'Winners and Losers in the Patent Wars Between Amazon, Google, Facebook, Apple, and Microsoft', <www.cbinsights.com/research/innovation-patents-apple-google-amazon-facebook-expert-intelligence>, 16 November 2017.

9   Soul Machines, 'Soul Machines Latest Project with Air New Zealand Shows the Potential of Digital Humans in Customer Service', <www.soulmachines.com/blog/airnewzealandandsoulmachines>, 26 September 2017.

10   Institute of Directors & ASB Bank, 'Director Sentiment Survey', IoD, 2017.

11   World Economic Forum, 'The Future of Jobs: Employment, skills and workforce strategy for the Fourth Industrial Revolution', Geneva: WEF, 2016.

12   Satya Nadella, 'The Partnership of the Future', <www.slate.com/articles/technology/future_tense/2016/06/microsoft_ceo_satya_nadella_humans_and_a_i_can_work_together_to_solve_society.html>, 28 June 2016.

13   Stuart Armstrong, Kaj Sotala & Seán S. ÓhÉigeartaigh, 'The Errors, Insights and Lessons of Famous AI Predictions—and What They Mean for the Future', <www.fhi.ox.ac.uk/wp-content/uploads/FAIC.pdf>, 20 May 2014.

14   Salim Ismail et al., *Exponential Organizations*, p. 33.

15   *Hays Global Skills Index 2017*, <www.hays.net.nz/global-skills-index/HAYS_128193>, 2017.

16   *Hays Global Skills Index 2017*.

17   James Manyika et al., 'Independent Work: Choice, necessity, and the gig economy', McKinsey Global Institute, <www.mckinsey.com/global-themes/employment-and-growth/independent-work-choice-necessity-and-the-gig-economy>, October 2016.

18   Ai Group Workforce Development, 'The Emergence of the Gig Economy', <cdn.aigroup.com.au/Reports/2016/Gig_Economy_August_2016.pdf>, August 2016.

19   Volvo Car Group, 'Volvo Cars to Supply Tens of Thousands of Autonomous Drive Compatible Cars to Uber', <www.media.volvocars.com/global/en-gb/media/pressreleases/216738/volvo-cars-to-supply-tens-of-thousands-of-autonomous-drive-compatible-cars-to-uber>, 20 November 2017.

20   Hamish Rutherford, 'Gig Economy Suppressing Wages More than Migration: Reserve Bank', <www.stuff.co.nz/business/95644204/gig-

economy-suppressing-wages-more-than-migration-reserve-bank>,
10 August 2017.

21   Klaus Schwab, 'The Fourth Industrial Revolution: What it means, how
to respond', <www.weforum.org/agenda/2016/01/the-fourth-industrial-
revolution-what-it-means-and-how-to-respond/>, 14 January 2016.

22   Jenny Soffel, 'What Are the 21st-Century Skills Every Student Needs?',
<www.weforum.org/agenda/2016/03/21st-century-skills-future-jobs-
students/>, 10 March 2016.

23   NZTalent, 'An Open Letter to the New Zealand Public', <https://nztalent.
org/>, 2017.

24   Universities New Zealand, 'No Qualification Required', <www.
universitiesnz.ac.nz/latest-news-and-publications/"no-qualification-
required", 31 October 2017.

25   Education Review, 'Nano Degrees: Friend or foe of the traditional
degree?', <archive.educationreview.co.nz/magazine/october-2014/
nanodegrees-friend-or-foe-of-the-traditional-degree/>, October 2014.

26   World Economic Forum, 'The Global Human Capital Report 2017:
Preparing people for the future of work', <www3.weforum.org/docs/WEF_
Global_Human_Capital_Report_2017.pdf>, 2017.

27   Chartered Accountants Australia and New Zealand and the New Zealand
Institute of Economic Research, 'Disruptive Technologies: Risks,
opportunities—Can New Zealand make the most of them?', Chartered
Accountants Australia and New Zealand, 2015.

28   Livia Gershon, 'The Automation-resistant Skills We Should Nurture',
<www.bbc.com/capital/story/20170726-the-automation-resistant-skills-
we-should-nurture>, 26 July 2017.

29   Thomas L. Friedman, 'From Hands to Heads to Hearts', <www.nytimes.
com/2017/01/04/opinion/from-hands-to-heads-to-hearts.html>,
4 January 2017.

30   Foundation for Young Australians, *The New Work Smarts: Thriving in the
new work order*, Sydney: FYA, 2017.

31   The Economist, 'Worldwide Educating for the Future Index: A
benchmark for the skills of tomorrow', The Economist Intelligence Unit,
2017.

32   John Gramlich, 'Most Americans Would Favor Policies to Limit Job
and Wage Losses Caused by Automation', <www.pewresearch.org/fact-
tank/2017/10/09/most-americans-would-favor-policies-to-limit-job-and-
wage-losses-caused-by-automation/>, 9 October 2017.

33 David Carey, 'Adapting to the Changing Labour Market in New Zealand', <www.oecd-ilibrary.org/economics/adapting-to-the-changing-labour-market-in-new-zealand_e6ced642-en>, 11 October 2017.

34 Mathew Boyd & Nick Wilson, 'Rapid Developments in Artificial Intelligence: How might the New Zealand government respond?', *Policy Quarterly*, 2017, vol. 13, no. 4, pp. 36–43.

35 Jacques-Pierre Dumas, 'Wellington Technology Group Create an AI Politician', <https://futurefive.co.nz/story/wellington-based-technology-group-create-ai-politician/>, 21 November 2017.

Chapter 3: Know yourself

1 Kevin Ashton, *How to Fly a Horse: The secret history of creation, invention and discovery*, New York: Doubleday, 2015, p. 59.

2 Scott Barry Kaufman, 'Confidence Matters Just as Much as Ability', *Psychology Today*, <www.psychologytoday.com/blog/beautiful-minds/201112/confidence-matters-just-much-ability>, 8 December 2011.

3 Ashton, *How to Fly a Horse*, p. 90.

4 Seth Godin is the author of a number of best-selling books including *Purple Cow* and *The Icarus Deception*; his blog can be seen at sethgodin.com/sg/.

Chapter 4: Know what's around you

1 'Digital in 2017: Australia, New Zealand & The Pacific', <www.slideshare.net/wearesocialsg/digital-in-2017-australia-new-zealand-the-pacific>, 26 January 2017.

2 Walter Quattrociocchi, Antonio Sacala & Cass R. Sunstein, 'Echo Chambers on Facebook', Discussion Paper No. 877, Cambridge, MA: Harvard Law School, 2016.

3 'Mothers asked nearly 300 questions a day, study finds', *The Telegraph*, <www.telegraph.co.uk/news/uknews/9959026/Mothers-asked-nearly-300-questions-a-day-study-finds.html>, 28 March 2013.

4 Todd B. Kashdan, 'Companies value curiosity but stifle it anyway', *Harvard Business Review*, <https://hbr.org/2015/10/companies-value-curiosity-but-stifle-it-anyway>, 21 October 2015.

5 Tony Seba is the co-founder of the independent think tank RethinkX; he is the author of a number of books, including *Clean Disruption of Energy*

and Transportation: How Silicon Valley will make oil, nuclear, natural gas, coal, electric utilities and conventional cars obsolete by 2030 (2014).

6   Brian Uzzi & Shannon Dunlop, 'How to Build your Network', *Harvard Business Review*, <https://hbr.org/2005/12/how-to-build-your-network>, 2005.

7   Alison Wood Brooks, Francesca Gino & Maurice Schweitzer, 'Smart People Ask For (My) Advice: Seeking advice boosts perceptions of competence', *Management Science*, 2015, vol. 61, no. 6.

8   Herminia Ibarra, Nancy M. Carter & Christine Silva, 'Why Men Still Get More Promotions Than Women', *Harvard Business Review*, <https://hbr.org/2010/09/why-men-still-get-more-promotions-than-women>, September 2010.

Chapter 5: Have a plan—and take chances

1   *Stanford Marshmallow Experiment*, <https://en.wikipedia.org/wiki/Stanford_marshmallow_experiment>.

2   B.J. Casey, Leah H. Somerville, Ian H. Gotlib et al., 'Behavioral and Neural Correlates of Delay of Gratification 40 Years Later', *Proceedings of the National Academy of Sciences of the United States of America*, <www.pnas.org/content/108/36/14998>, 2011.

3   Elliot D. Cohen, 'The fear of losing control', *Psychology Today*, <www.psychologytoday.com/blog/what-would-aristotle-do/201105/the-fear-losing-control>, 22 May 2011.

4   Richard N. Bolles, *What Color Is Your Parachute? A practical manual for job-hunters and career-changers.* First published in 1972, the book has been revised and reissued almost every year since.

5   Mary Morrissey, 'The power of writing down your goals and dreams', *HuffPost*, <www.huffingtonpost.com/marymorrissey/the-power-of-writing-down_b_12002348.html>, 6 December 2017.

6   See *Morning Pages*, <http://juliacameronlive.com/basic-tools/morning-pages/>.

7   Barney G. Glaser & Anselm L. Strauss, *The Discovery of Grounded Theory: Strategies for qualitative research* (1st edn 1967), New Brunswick/London: Transaction Publishers, 2009.

Chapter 6: Look after yourself

1   WorkSafe New Zealand, 'Healthy Work: Worksafe's strategic plan for work-related health 2016 to 2026', Wellington: WorkSafe New Zealand, 2016.

2   Workplace Health and Safety Queensland, 'Health and Wellbeing at Work', <www.worksafe.qld.gov.au/injury-prevention-safety/health-and-wellbeing-at-work/>, 2017.

3   WorkSafe New Zealand, 'Healthy Work'.

4   Hugh Schofield, 'The Plan to Ban Emails Out of Hours', *BBC News*, <www.bbc.com/news/magazine-36249647>, 11 May 2016.

5   Rich Fernandez, '5 Ways to Boost Your Resilience At Work', *Harvard Business Review*, <https://hbr.org/2016/06/627-building-resilience-ic-5-ways-to-build-your-personal-resilience-at-work>, 27 June 2016.

6   Andrea Ovans, 'What Resilience Means, and Why It Matters', *Harvard Business Review*, <https://hbr.org/2015/01/what-resilience-means-and-why-it-matters>, 5 January 2015.

7   Ovans, 'What Resilience Means, and Why It Matters'.

8   Shawn Achor & Michelle Gielan, 'Resilience Is About How You Recharge, Not How You Endure', *Harvard Business Review*, <https://hbr.org/2016/06/resilience-is-about-how-you-recharge-not-how-you-endure>, 24 June 2016.

9   Bradley Hook, 'The Benefits of Learning Resilience', The Resilience Institute, <https://resiliencei.com/2017/08/benefits-learning-resilience/>, 10 August 2017.

10   See www.friendsresilience.org/; https://allright.org.nz/tools/sparklers/; http://livingwell.org.nz/.

11   Anna Kwek, Huong T. Bui, John Rynne & Kevin So, 'The Impacts of Self-esteem and Resilience on Academic Performance: An investigation of domestic and international hospitality and tourism undergraduate students',
Journal of Hospitality & Tourism Education, 2013, vol. 25, no. 3, pp. 110–122, <https://experts.griffith.edu.au/publication/n00e6a43b6a4300740d1ed19f84b86e04>.

12   Careers New Zealand, 'Student Career Management Competencies', <www.careers.govt.nz/assets/pages/docs/tertiary-student-career-management-competencies.pdf>, 2012.

13   See www.likeminds.org.nz.

Chapter 7: Bring on the future

1   Attributed variously to baseball player Yogi Berra, poet Paul Valéry, science-fiction writer Arthur C. Clarke and Apple founder Steve Jobs.

2   'Medieval helpdesk with English subtitles', <www.youtube.com/watch?v=pQHX-SjgQvQ>.

3   Kathleen Elkins, 'Mark Zuckerberg Shares the Best Piece of Advice Peter Thiel Ever Gave Him', CNBC.com, <www.cnbc.com/2016/08/25/mark-zuckerberg-shares-the-best-piece-of-advice-peter-thiel-ever-gave-him.html>, 25 August 2016.

SELECT BIBLIOGRAPHY

Full details of all the works referenced in the text are included in the Notes; this Select Bibliography lists the most significant of these, and additional works that readers might find helpful.

Work, but not as we know it

Chartered Accountants Australia and New Zealand and the New Zealand Institute of Economic Research, 'Disruptive Technologies: Risks, opportunities—Can New Zealand make the most of them?', Chartered Accountants Australia and New Zealand, 2015

Colvin, Geoff, *Humans are Underrated: What high achievers know that brilliant machines never will*, New York: Portfolio/Penguin, 2015

Frey, Carl Benedikt & Osborne, Michael A., 'The Future of Employment: How susceptible are jobs to computerisation?', Working Paper, Oxford, UK: Oxford Martin Programme on Technology and Employment, University of Oxford, 2013

Friedman, Stewart D., *Leading the Life You Want: Skills for integrating work and life*, Boston, MA: Harvard Business Review Press, 2014

Friedman, Thomas L., *The World Is Flat: A brief history of the twenty-first century*, New York: Farrar, Straus and Giroux, 2005

Institute of Directors, 'Director Sentiment Survey', <www.iod.org.nz/Governance-Resources/Publications/Director-Sentiment-Survey>, 2017

Ismail, Salim, with Michael S. Malone & Yuri van Geest, *Exponential Organizations: Why new organizations are ten times better, faster and cheaper than yours (and what to do about it)*, New York: Diversion Books, 2014

Kaplan, Jerry, *Humans Need Not Apply: A guide to wealth and work in the age of artificial intelligence*, New Haven, CT: Yale University Press, 2015

Sheninger, Eric C., *Digital Leadership: Changing paradigms for changing times*, Thousand Oaks, CA: SAGE Publications Inc., 2014

World Economic Forum, 'The Future of Jobs: Employment, skills and workforce strategy for the Fourth Industrial Revolution', Global Challenge Insight Report, Geneva: WEF, 2016

Automation and artificial intelligence

Armstrong, Stuart et al., 'The Errors, Insights and Lessons of Famous AI Predictions—and what they mean for the Future', <www.fhi.ox.ac.uk/wp-content/uploads/FAIC.pdf>, 2014

Boyd, Matthew & Wilson, Nick, 'Rapid developments in artificial intelligence: How might the New Zealand government respond?' *Policy Quarterly*, 2017, vol. 13, no. 4

Christensen, Clayton M., *The Innovator's Dilemma: When new technologies cause great firms to fail*, Boston, MA: Harvard Business School Press, 1997

Deloitte, '2017 Deloitte Global Human Capital Trends: Rewriting the rules for the digital age', <www2.deloitte.com/content/dam/Deloitte/us/Documents/human-capital/hc-2017-global-human-capital-trends-us.pdf>, 2017

Ford, Martin, *The Rise of the Robots: Technology and the threat of mass unemployment*, London: Oneworld Publications, 2015

Kelly, Kevin, *The Inevitable: Understanding the 12 technological forces that will shape our future*, New York: Penguin Random House, 2016

Manyika, James et al., 'Harnessing Automation for a Future That Works', McKinsey Global Institute report, <www.mckinsey.com/global-themes/digital-disruption/harnessing-automation-for-a-future-that-works>, 2017

Meffert, J. & Swaminathan, A., *Digital @ Scale: The playbook you need to transform your company*, New York: John Wiley & Sons Inc., 2017

The gig economy

Ai Group Workforce Development, 'The Emergence of the Gig Economy', <cdn.aigroup.com.au/Reports/2016/Gig_Economy_August_2016.pdf>, 2016

Carey, David, 'Adapting to the Changing Labour Market in New Zealand', <www.oecd-ilibrary.org/economics/adapting-to-the-changing-labour-market-in-new-zealand_e6ced642-en>, 2017

Foundation for Young Australians, *The New Work Mindset*, Sydney: FYA, 2017

Foundation for Young Australians, *The New Work Smarts: Thriving in the new work order*, Sydney: FYA, 2017

Manyika, James et al., 'Independent Work: Choice, necessity, and the gig economy', <www.mckinsey.com/global-themes/employment-and-growth/independent-work-choice-necessity-and-the-gig-economy>, 2016

World Economic Forum, 'The Future of Jobs: Employment, skills and workforce strategy for the Fourth Industrial Revolution', Global Challenge Insight Report, Geneva: WEF, 2016

Reinventing learning

Ashton, Kevin, *How to Fly a Horse: The secret history of creation, invention and discovery*, New York: Doubleday, 2015

Careers New Zealand, 'Student Career Management Competencies', <www.careers.govt.nz/assets/pages/docs/tertiary-student-career-management-competencies.pdf>, 2012

Foundation for Young Australians, *The New Basics: Big data reveals the skills young people need for the New Work Order*, Sydney: FYA, 2017

Fullan, Michael, *Stratosphere: Integrating technology, pedagogy, and change knowledge*, Boston, MA: Pearson Education, 2012

The Economist, 'Worldwide Educating for the Future Index: A benchmark for the skills of tomorrow', The Economist Intelligence Unit, 2017

World Economic Forum, 'The Global Human Capital Report 2017: Preparing people for the future of work', <www3.weforum.org/docs/WEF_Global_Human_Capital_Report_2017.pdf>, 2017

Know yourself

Casey, B.J. et al., 'Behavioral and neural correlates of delay of gratification 40 years later', *Proceedings of the National Academy of Sciences of the United States of America*, <www.pnas.org/content/108/36/14988>, 2011

Cohen, Elliot D., 'The fear of losing control', *Psychology Today*, <www.psychologytoday.com/blog/what-would-aristotle-do/201105/the-fear-losing-control>, 2011

Fields, Jonathan, *Uncertainty: Turning fear and doubt into fuel for brilliance*, New York: Portfolio/Penguin, 2011

Gallup Press, *First, Break All the Rules: What the world's greatest managers do differently*, Omaha, NE: Gallup Press, 2016

Glaser, Barney G. & Strauss, Anselm L., *The Discovery of Grounded Theory: Strategies for qualitative research* (1st edn 1967), New Brunswick/London: Transaction Publishers, 2009

Kahneman, Daniel, *Thinking, Fast and Slow*, New York: Farrar, Straus and Giroux, 2011

Kaufman, Scott Barry, 'Confidence matters just as much as ability', *Psychology Today*, <www.psychologytoday.com/blog/beautiful-minds/201112/confidence-matters-just-much-ability>, 2011

Light, Larry, 'The Real Reason People Don't Save for Retirement', <www.forbes.com/sites/lawrencelight/2016/02/24/the-real-reason-people-dont-save-for-retirement/#71ea2e737c5c>, 2016

Locke, Edwin & Latham, Gary, 'New directions in goal-setting theory', *Current Directions in Psychological Science*, 2017, vol. 15, no. 5

Know what's around you

Kashdan, Todd B., 'Companies value curiosity but stifle it anyway', *Harvard Business Review*, <https://hbr.org/2015/10/companies-value-curiosity-but-stifle-it-anyway>, 2015

Quattrociocchi, Walter et al., 'Echo Chambers on Facebook', Discussion Paper No. 877, Cambridge, MA: Harvard Law School, 2016

Uzzi, Brian & Dunlop, Shannon, 'How to build your network', *Harvard Business Review*, <https://hbr.org/2005/12/how-to-build-your-network>, 2005

Wood Brooks, Alison et al., 'Smart people ask for (my) advice: Seeking advice boosts perceptions of competence', *Management Science*, 2015, vol. 61, no. 6

Look after yourself

Achor, Shawn & Gielan, Michelle, 'Resilience is about how you recharge, not how you endure', *Harvard Business Review*, <https://hbr.org/2016/06/resilience-is-about-how-you-recharge-not-how-you-endure>, 2016

Fernandez, Rich, '5 ways to boost your resilience at work', *Harvard Business Review*, <https://hbr.org/2016/06/627-building-resilience-ic-5-ways-to-build-your-personal-resilience-at-work>, 2016

Fields, Jonathan, *Uncertainty: Turning fear and doubt into fuel for brilliance*, New York: Portfolio/Penguin, 2011

Gratton, Lynda & Scott, Andrew, *The 100-Year Life: Living and working in an age of longevity*, London: Bloomsbury, 2016

Ovans, Andrea, 'What resilience means, and why it matters', *Harvard Business Review*, <https://hbr.org/2015/01/what-resilience-means-and-why-it-matters>, 2015

Workplace Health and Safety Queensland, 'Health and Wellbeing at Work', <www.worksafe.qld.gov.au/injury-prevention-safety/health-and-wellbeing-at-work/>, 2017

WorkSafe New Zealand, 'Healthy Work: Worksafe's strategic plan for work-related health 2016 to 2026', Wellington: WorkSafe New Zealand, 2016

INDEX